Paul Bowles was born in New York and came to Europe in 1931 to study music with Aaron Copland. In 1938 he married Jane Auer, herself a gifted writer who was to achieve literary fame. After the war they settled in Tangier, which is now Paul Bowles' permanent home.

Also in Abacus by the same author:

Paul Bowles

THEIR HEADS ARE GREEN

AN ABACUS BOOK

First published in Great Britain by Peter Owen Publishers Ltd 1963
Published by Sphere Books in Abacus 1990
1st reprint 1990

Far and few, far and few,
Are the lands where the Jumblies live;
Their heads are green and their hands are blue,
And they went to sea in a Sieve.
EDWARD LEAR

Printed in England by Clays Ltd, St Ives plc

ISBN 0 3491 0155 8

Sphere Books Ltd
A Division of
Macdonald & Co (Publishers) Ltd
Orbit House, 1 New Fetter Lane, London EC4A 1AR
A member of Maxwell Macmillan Pergamon Publishing Corporation

CONTENTS

INTRODUCTION

Each time I go to a place I have not seen before, I hope it will be as different as possible from the places I already know. I assume it is natural for a traveller to seek diversity, and that it is the human element which gives him the strongest impression of difference. If people and their manner of living were alike everywhere, there would not be much point in moving from one place to another. With few exceptions, landscape alone is of insufficient interest to warrant the effort it takes to see it. Even the works of man, unless they are being used in his daily living, have a way of losing their meaning, and take on the qualities of decoration. What makes Istanbul worthwhile to the outsider is not the presence of the mosques and the covered souks, but the fact that they still function as such. If the people of India did not have their remarkable awareness of the importance of spiritual discipline, it would be an overwhelmingly depressing country to visit, notwithstanding its architectural wonders. And North Africa without its tribes, inhabited by, let us say, the Swiss, would be merely a rather more barren California.

The concept of the *status quo* is a purely theoretical one; modifications occur hourly. It would be an absurdity to expect any group of people to maintain its present characteristics or manner of living. But the visitor to a place whose charm is a result of its backwardness is inclined to hope it will remain that way, regardless of how those who live in it may feel. The seeker of the picturesque sees the spread of improved techniques as an unalloyed abomination. Still, there are much worse things.

M. Claude Levi-Strauss, the anthropologist, claims that in order for the Western world to continue to function properly it must constantly get rid of vast quantities of waste matter, which it inflicts on less fortunate peoples. "What travel discloses to us first of all is our own garbage, flung in the face of humanity."

At the other end of the ideological spectrum are those who regard any objective description of things as they are today in an underdeveloped country as imperialist propaganda. Having been

7

subjected to attack from both camps, I am aware that such countries are a delicate subject to write about. With reference to one of the pieces in this volume (*Fish Traps and Private Business*) a British resident of Ceylon declared: "Other authors have found peace and beauty here in the simple life of our coolies". Whereas, when I wrote *Mustapha and His Friends*, a strong-minded French lady translated it into her language, had two hundred copies mimeographed, and distributed them among Moslem politicians to illustrate the typical reactionary attitude of Americans toward oppressed peoples.

My own belief is that the people of the alien cultures are being ravaged not so much by the by-products of our civilization, as by the irrational longing on the part of members of their own educated minorities to cease being themselves and become Westerners. The various gadget-forms of our "garbage" make convenient fetishes to assist in achieving the magic transformation. But there is a difference between allowing an organism to evolve naturally and trying to force the change. Many post-colonial regimes attempt to hasten the process of Europeanization by means of campaigns and decrees. Coercion can destroy the traditional patterns of thought, it is true, but what is needed is that they be transformed into viable substitute patterns, and this can be done only empirically by the people themselves. A cultural vacuum is not even productive of national-ism, which at least involves a certain consciousness of identity.

Since human behaviour is becoming everywhere less differen-tiated, the Jumblie hunters are having to increase the radius of their searches and lower their standards. For a man to qualify as a Jumblie today he need not practice anthropophagy or infibulation; it is enough for him to sacrifice a coconut or bury a packet of curses in his neighbour's garden. It may be, says W. H. Auden, "that in a not remote future, it will be impossible to distinguish human beings living on one area of the earth's surface from those living on any other". It is comforting to imagine that when that day arrives we may be in a position to have the inhabitants of a nearby planet as our Jumblies. There is always the possibility, too, that they may have us as theirs. P.B. 1963.

FISH TRAPS AND PRIVATE BUSINESS •

—Welideniya Estate, Ceylon

The landscape is restless, – a sea of disorderly hills rising steeply. In all directions it looks the same. The hills are sharp bumps with a thin, hairy vegetation that scarcely covers them. Most of this is rubber, and the rubber is wintering. Mr. Murrow, the planter, says that in another week or two the present brownish yellow leaves will be replaced by new ones. Where the rubber stops the tea begins. There the earth looks raw. The rocks show between the low bushes; here and there a mulberry tree with lopped branches, planted for shade.

On top of one of these steep humps is the bungalow, spread out all along the crest. Directly below to the southwest, almost straight down, is the river with its sandy banks. But in between, the steep declivity is terraced with tea, and by day the voices of the Tamil pickers are constantly audible. At night there are fires outside the huts on the opposite bank of the river.

The air is hot and breathless, the only respite coming in the middle of the afternoon, when it rains. And afterward, when it has stopped, one has very little energy until night falls. However, by then it is too late to do anything but talk or read. The lights work on the tea-factory circuit. When everyone is in bed, Mr. Murrow calls from under his mosquito-net through the open door of his bedroom to a Tamil waiting outside on the lawn. Five minutes later all the lights slowly die, and the house is in complete darkness save for the small oil lamps on the shelves in the bathrooms. Nothing is locked. The bedrooms have swinging shutters like old-fashioned bar-room doors, that reach to within two feet of the floor. The windows have no glass, – only curtains of very thin silk. All night long a barefoot watchman shouldering a military rifle pads round and round the bungalow. Sometimes, when it is too hot to sleep, I get up and sit out on the verandah. Once there was no air

9

even there, and I moved a chair to the lawn. On his first trip around then, the watchman saw me, and made a grunting sound which I interpreted as one of disapproval. It may not have been; I don't know.

The nights seem endless, perhaps because I lie awake listening to the unfamiliar sounds made by the insects, birds and reptiles. By now I can tell more or less how late it is by the section of the nocturnal symphony that has been reached. In the early evening there are things that sound like cicadas. Later the geckos begin. (There is a whole science of divination based on the smallest details of the behaviour of these little lizards; while the household is still up they scurry silently along the walls and ceiling catching insects, and it is only well on into the night that they begin to call out, from one side of the room to the other.) Still later there is a noise like a rather rasping katydid. By three in the morning everything has stopped but a small bird whose cry is one note of pure tone and unvarying pitch. There seem always to be two of these in the rain-tree outside my room; they take great care to sing antiphonally, and the one's voice is exactly a whole tone above the other's. Sometimes in the morning Mrs. Murrow asks me if I heard the cobra sing during the night. I have never been able to answer in the affirmative, because in spite of her description, ("like a silver coin falling against a rock") I have no clear idea of what to listen for.

We drink strong, dark tea six or seven times a day. No pretext is needed for Mr. Murrow to ring the bell and order it. Often when it seems perfectly good to me, he will send it back with the complaint that it has been poorly brewed. All the tea consumed in the bungalow is top-leaf tea, hand-picked by Mr. Murrow himself. He maintains that there is none better in the world, and I am forced to agree that it tastes like a completely different beverage from any tea I have had before.

The servants enter the rooms bowing so low that their backs form an arch, and their hands are held above their heads in an attitude of prayer. Last night I happened to go into the dining room a few minutes before dinner, and old Mrs. Van Dort, Mrs. Murrow's mother, was already seated at her place. The oldest servant, Siringam, suddenly appeared in the doorway of the verandah leading to the kitchen, bent over double with his hands above his head, announcing the entrance of a kitchen-maid bearing the dog's meal. The woman carried the dish to the old lady, who sternly inspected it, and then commanded her in Sinhalese to put it down in a corner for the animal. "I must always look at the dog's food," she told me, "otherwise the servants eat part of it and the poor dog grows thinner and thinner."

"But are the servants that hungry?"

"Certainly not!" she cried. "But they like the dog's food better than their own."

Mrs. Murrow's son by a former marriage came to spend last night, bringing his Sinhalese wife with him; she had already told me at some length of how she resisted the marriage for three years because of the girl's blood. Mrs. Murrow is of the class which calls itself *burgher*, claiming an unbroken line of descendency from the Dutch settlers of two centuries ago. I have yet to see a Burgher who looks Caucasian, the admixture of Sinhalese being always perfectly discernible. It is significant that the Burghers feel compelled to announce their status to newcomers; the apparent reason is to avoid being taken for "natives". The tradition, however, is that they are Europeans, and one must accept it without question. The son is a tall, gentle man who wears a grey cassock and keeps his hands folded tightly all the time, a habit which makes him look as though he were prey to a constant inner anguish. He is a minister of the Anglican church, but this does not keep him from being of the extreme left politically. His joy is to stir up dissension among his parishioners by delivering sermons in which Communists are depicted as holding high posts in Heaven. He has told me some amusing anecdotes of his life as a teacher in the outlying provinces before he was ordained. Of these the ones I remember have to do with the strange faculty the children have for speaking passable English without knowing the meaning of the words they use. One boy, upon being asked to answer which he would prefer to be, a tailor or a lawyer, was unable to reply. "You know what a tailor is, don't you?" said Mr. Clasen. The boy said he did, and he also knew the functions of a lawyer, but he could not answer the question. "But why?" insisted Mr. Clasen, thinking that perhaps some recondite bit of Buddhist philosophy was about to be forthcoming. But the boy finally said: "I know tailor and I know lawyer, but please, sir, what is be?" Another boy wrote: "The horse is a noble animal, but when irritated will not do so."

When you ask a question of a Sinhalese who does not know English, he is likely to react in a most curious fashion. First he looks swiftly at you, then he looks away, his features retreating into an expression of pleasant contemplation, as if your voice were an agreeable but distant memory that he had just recalled and thought it worthwhile to savour briefly. After a few seconds of giving himself up to this inward satisfaction he goes on about his business without ever looking your way again, – not even if you insist, or wait a bit and make your inquiry afresh. You have become invisible. At the rest-houses in the country, where the members of the personnel feel they must put up some sort of front, they say: "Oh, oh, oh," in a commiserating tone, (*oh* is *yes*) as if they understood only too well, and were forbearing to say more for the sake of decorum. Then they wag their heads back and forth, from side to side, a gesture which reminds you of a metronome going rather too quickly, keeping their bright eyes on you, listening politely until you have finished speaking, when they smile beautifully and walk away. The servants who do speak English insist upon calling you "Master", which is disconcerting because it seems to imply responsibility of some sort on your part. They also use the third person instead of the second: "Master wishing eat now?" The youngest generation, however, has almost unanimously adopted the more neutral "sir", (pronounced "sar") as a substitute for the too colonial-sounding "master".

There is a long, thin, green adder that likes to lie in the sun on top of the tea bushes; one of these bit a woman recently while she was picking. Mr. Murrow hurried to the scene, and taking up a pruning knife, cut off the tip of her finger, applying crystals of potassium permanganate to the flesh. She was saved in this way, but as soon as she regained consciousness, she immediately went to the police and filed a complaint, accusing Mr. Murrow of causing irreparable damage to her finger. When the investigator came to the estate, he heard the details of the case, and told the woman that thanks to Mr. Murrow's quick action she was still alive; without it she would have been dead. The woman's husband, who was present at the hearing, jumped up and drew a knife on the investigator, but was prevented from hurting him. When they had subdued the man, he wailed across at the investigator: "You have no sense! I could have collected plenty of rupees for that finger, and I would have given you half."

The public toilets in the villages, instead of being marked LADIES or WOMEN, bear signs that read: URINALS FOR FEMALES.

A sign on the side of a building in Akmimana: WEDDING CAKES AND OTHER THING SUPPLIED FOR WEDDINGS IN CONVENIENT TIMES.

Another, in Colombo: DR. RAO'S TONIC – A DIVINE DRUG.

A Burgher who works in the travel agency of the Grand Oriental Hotel and who had seen me when I first arrived, said to me a few weeks later when I stopped in: "You're losing your colour." "What?" I cried incredulously. "After all this time in the sun? I'm five shades darker than I was." He looked confused, but continued patiently: "That's what I say. You're losing your colour."

—Kaduwela

The Lunawa rest-house was a disagreeable place to stay, directly opposite the railway station in the middle of a baking and unshaded patch of dried-up lawn. In the concrete cell I was given it was impossible to shut out the sounds made by the other guests, who happened to be extremely noisy. The room next to mine was occupied by a party of eight men, who spent the entire afternoon and evening giggling and guffawing. When I would walk past their door I could see them lying in their sarongs across the two beds which they had pushed together. In the dining room the radio never ceased blaring at maximum volume. The food was ghastly, and there was no mosquito net available for my bed, and therefore

13

no protection against the tiny insects that constantly brushed against my face in the dark, seeking to get under the sheet with me. When I finally got into the state of nerves they had been trying to induce, I jumped up, dressed, and rushed out, to the horror of the boy lying on his mat across the front doorway. He too sprang up, went to an inner room to fetch the keeper, and together they cried out after me across the dark lawn: "Master going?"

"Coming back, coming back!" I called, and began to walk quickly up the road toward the lagoon. When I got to the bridge I stood a while. The water was absolutely still, and there were dozens of pinkish flames guttering in lamps placed just at the surface, each with its unmoving reflection. And each lamp illumined a complex scaffolding of bamboo poles; these pale constructions scattered across the black expanse of water looked like precarious altars, and the fact that I knew they were fish-traps made them no less extraordinary, no less beautiful. To break the silence a drum began to beat on the far shore. Presently a man came riding by on a bicycle; as he passed me he turned his flashlight into my face. The sight of me standing in that spot startled him, and he pedalled madly away across the bridge.

I walked on to Lunawa Junction where I stood in the road listening to a radio in a corner "hotel" play Tamil music. (What the Sinhalese call hotels are merely tea-houses with three or four tables and a tiny space behind a screen or partition where there are mats on the floor for those who wish to rest.) People wandered past now and then and stared at me; I was clearly an object of great interest. Europeans never appear at night in such places. When I sat down on a culvert I was soon the centre of a semicircle of men, some clad only in G-strings, and with hair that reached half-way down their backs. It was no use talking to me in Sinhalese, but they went right on trying. One who spoke English finally arrived and asked me if I would like to race him down the road. I declined, saying I was tired. This was true: it was after midnight, and I was beginning to wish there were some comfortable place in the neighbourhood where I could lay my head. The English-speaking man then told me that they had all been asleep, but had got up because someone had arrived with the news that a stranger was standing in the road. While I sat there doing my best to make some sort of polite conversation, three older men in white robes came by, and seeing the crowd, stopped. These were obviously of a higher social station, and they were most disapproving of what they saw. One of them who had rapidly been delegated as spokesman stepped forward, indicated the band of wild-eyed, long-haired individuals, and said: "Hopeless people." I pretended not to understand, whereupon all three set to work repeating the same words over and over, accenting equally each syllable. I was so fascinated with their performance that nearly all the nudists had disappeared into the dark before I realized they were leaving, and all at once I was sitting there facing only these three serious, chanting men. "Come," said the leader, and he took me by the arm and helped me up, – I won't say *forcing* me to walk, because his firmness was expressed with too much gentleness for that – but seeing to it that I did walk, with him and his friends, back to the road intersection where bats dipped in the air under the one streetlight. "Now you go to rest house," he said, showing that he knew more English than the two-word refrain which had sufficed him until then. But then a second later, "Hopeless people," he sang, and the others, looking still more grave beneath the light, agreed with him once more. Lamely I protested that I should go back presently, when I felt like it, but they were adamant; it was clear that my personal desires were quite beside the point. They called to a boy who stood under a tree near the "hotel", and charged him to walk the mile with me back to the rest house. For perhaps a minute I argued, half laughingly, half seriously, and then I turned and started up the road. They called good-night, and went on their way. The boy kept close beside me, partly out of fear, I imagine, and when I got to the bridge and stood still for a moment to look at the water and the lights, he pressed me to go on quickly, pretending there were crocodiles in the lagoon and that they came out of the water at night. I don't think he believed it at all, but he wanted to accomplish his mission and get to the safety of the rest house as fast as he could. (Trees harbour spirits here; the older and larger ones have niches carved into their trunks where the people put long-burning altar candles. The flickering lights attract the spirits, like moths, and keep them from leaving the tree and doing harm beyond its immediate vicinity.) At the rest house the man and the boy were waiting up for me. My road companion had no intention of augmenting his ordeal by going back across the lagoon unaccompanied; he curled up on the floor of the verandah and spent the night there. The gigglers had gone to sleep and there was quiet at last, but the insects were more numerous and active than they had been earlier. I did not have a very successful night.

I had already made arrangements to spend the next night at Homagama, where the rest house is, (or at least appears to be,) somewhat superior. When the elderly rest house keeper showed me his rooms there, he tried to get me to take an extension of the dining room, on the pretext that it would be quieter. The only other available room was next to his quarters, and that, he said apologetically, he was sure Master would not like at all. Since the room he was trying to give me had only three complete walls, the fourth being merely a wooden screen about five feet high over which I could see two gentlemen drinking ginger beer at a table, I unwisely decided upon the room adjoining his quarters. Once I was settled with my luggage partially unpacked, and the servants had hung the mosquito-net and brought in a very feeble oil lamp, I discovered my error. This room also was only a section of another room; in the part not inhabited by me a baby began to wail, and presently the voice of an extremely old woman rose in incantation. Whether it was a lullaby, a prayer, or merely a senile lamentation, I am still too unfamiliar with the culture of the land to tell. But it went on intermittently until dawn when the sounds of the poultry, the crows in the mango trees, and the locomotives which passed by the doorway, blotted it out. Whenever the old lady would stop, the infant would wake her up; as soon as the baby ceased crying, she would start afresh and awaken the baby.

In the morning I discovered that there was a third room, but that it was due to be occupied any moment by what is euphemistically called a "honeymoon couple". At six thirty in the morning they arrived, and when they had left in the late afternoon, I was allowed to take it. It was vastly better, and I kept it for the next two nights, much to the keeper's disgust, since he had to put all the couples that arrived during that time into the other rooms. Given the fact that by far the larger part of his personal revenue comes in the form of gratuities from such parties, it is understandable that he should like to provide them with the best accomodations. (Another expression used by rest house keepers to refer to their honeymoon couples is "private business". Those concerned do not sign their names in the register, and for that privilege leave relatively large tips. The keeper at Kesbewa informed me that his rooms were all reserved for private business for the next six weeks.)

During the late afternoon of the third day I had to leave. Unless one has special permission from the government to remain longer, one's stay in a rest house is strictly limited to three nights, which is presumably ample time for whatever private business one may wish to conduct.

I engaged a bullock-cart with the body of an old-fashioned buggy, drawn by a small beige-coloured zebu, and with the driver, who had never heard the English words "yes" and "no", started along the back roads through the forest for Kaduela. There were a good many small villages on the way, at one of which we had to stop so that the luggage, which was constantly slipping and falling out into the dust, could be rearranged and tied more securely. The driver bought a great length of thick but feeble rope for the purpose, and we went ahead. The incredible jolting became unbearable after a while; I had pains everywhere from my knees to my neck. The rope of course kept breaking, and the valises continued to slip and fall out. The charm of the landscape however had induced in me such a complete euphoria that nothing mattered. I only wanted it to stay light as long as possible so I could go on being aware of my surroundings. The forest was not constant; it opened again and again onto wide stretches of green paddy field where herons waded. Each time we plunged again into the woods it was darker, until finally I could no longer distinguish areca palms from bamboo. People walking along the road were carrying torches made of palm leaves bound tightly together, that burned with a fierce red flame; they held them high above their heads, and the sparks dropped behind them all along the way. In one village cinnamon bark had been piled against the houses. The odour enveloped the whole country-side. Now every ten minutes or so the driver stopped, got down, and put a new wax taper into one or the other of the two lamps at the sides of the buggy. It was very late when we got to Kaduwela.

Here the rest house is on the river, the Kelani Ganga, which flows by at the base of the rocks, just a few feet below the verandah. At night in the quiet I can sometimes hear a slight gurgle out there, but I am never sure whether it is a fish or merely the current. Occasionally a whole string of bamboo barges floats swiftly by without a sound; if one did not see the moving red spots, the braziers where the members of the crew are cooking their food, one would not know it was there.

—Hikkaduwa

In Ceylon the Christmas-tree light is a favourite decoration. They use thousands of them at once, string them across the fronts of the houses and shops, through the trees, and up and down the dagobas of the temples. If there is a religious procession, whatever is carried through the streets is covered with coloured electric bulbs. During Perahera in Kandy as many as eighty elephants parade at night, wearing strings of lights; they take the place of the emeralds, rubies and diamonds that cover the beasts in the daytime processions. Last week while I was there in Kandy the Moslems had a festival. They carried a pagoda-like tower through the streets, every square inch of whose area was ablaze with tiny coloured lights. It looked rather like a colossal, glittering wedding cake. I followed it up and down Trincomalee Street and Ward Street, and then I went to bed. Until then I had not realized that there was a mosque across the garden from my room, (they seem to have dispensed with muezzins here, – at least, one never hears them) but that evening there was magnificent music coming from a courtyard behind the mosque. It went on all night, like a soft wind in the trees. I listened until nearly three from my bed, and then it carried me off into sleep.

Last night there was a *pirith* ceremony at a house across the road. The family that lived next door to the one holding the ceremony had offered their verandah for the installation of a generator, for there had to be electric light and a great deal of it. So, the clanking of the motor all but covered the chanting of the men. In one corner of the main room they had built a small cubicle. Its walls were of translucent paper, cut into designs along the edges of the partitions, so that each section looked like the frame of a fancy valentine. There were lights everywhere, but the greatest amount of light came from inside the cubicle. Earlier in the evening I had noticed two men winding or unwinding a white silk thread between them; now there was a decanter full of an unidentified liquid on the table, and the thread connected its neck with a part of the ceiling that was invisible from where I stood. The table was surrounded by men sitting pressed close to one another, chanting. One of the onlookers who stood with me in the road pointed out to me that the chanting was being done in Pali, not in Sinhalese. As if it were necessary to excuse the use of such an ancient language, he added that Catholic services were conducted in Latin, not in English, and I said I quite understood.

The Sinhalese are beyond a doubt one of the least musical people in the world. It would be quite impossible to have less sense of pitch, line or rhythm. There was thus no way of my knowing whether the sounds they were making were meant to have any definite pitch and to consist of a series of separate, articulated tones, or whether they are supposed only to be uttered in a non-naturalistic manner, simply to distinguish them from the tones used in ordinary speech. That is to say, there would be no way of knowing those things unless one had heard them try to sing definite melodies, such as *Sri Lanka*, their present national anthem. But when one has seen on what a vast scale can be their failure to carry even three consecutive tones, one realizes that there can be few societies on earth less aware of music and less capable of producing any.

I asked what the white silk thread meant, and was told that it was decoration, but since everything in the ceremony had been arranged with show-window precision, and since the thread, shooting upward at its crazy angle toward the ceiling, was clearly not an adornment to anything, I was not inclined to accept that version of its function. The men shouted in a desperate fashion, so that they were obliged to lean against the table for support. All night long they kept it up. When I awoke at quarter to five they were still at it, but the sound now had a different contour; one could say that in a way it had subsided, being now a succession of short wails with a tessitura never exceeding a major third, a sequence that repeated itself exactly, again and again, with no variation. (I was told today that the *pirith* chant is allowed four distinct tones, – no more, since the addition of a fifth would put it into the category of music, which is strictly forbidden. Perhaps the celebrants are too much preoccupied with observing the letter of the law. In any case, within the allowed gamut they hit every quarter-tone they could find.) The dogs of the rest house objected now and them with howls and yapping, until the guard would silence them with a shout.

A young Buddhist who had been standing outside the house while I was there offered to explain a few details about the ceremony to me. "You see the women?" he said. They were sitting in the outer part of the room, conversing quietly. "They are not allowed inside." The chanting begins, he said, (in this case it was at nine in the evening,) with all the men shouting together. Then as they tire, only the two strongest continue, while the others gather their forces. At daybreak once again everyone joins in, after six hours or so of alternating shifts. Purpose of the ceremony: to keep evil in abeyance. The young man did not hold the custom in very high esteem, and suggested that I visit a monastery four miles away on an island where the *bhikkus* behaved in a really correct manner. Even Buddhism is riddled with primitive practices. Practically speaking, the *pirith* is merely a quiet variation of devil-dancing.

—Colombo

The Pettah is the only part of the city where the visitor can get even a faint idea of what life in Colombo might have been like before the Twentieth Century's gangrene set in. It is at the end of a long and unrewarding walk across the railroad tracks and down endless unshaded streets, and no one in Ceylon seems to be able to understand how I can like it. It is customary to assume an expression of slight disgust when one pronounces the word *Pettah*.

The narrow streets are jammed with zebu-drawn drays which naked coolies (no one ever says *labourers*) are loading and unloading. Scavenging crows scream and chuckle in the gutters. The shops specialize in unexpected merchandise: some sell nothing but fireworks, or religious chromolithographs depicting incidents in the lives of Hindu gods, or sarongs, or incense. With no arcades and no trees the heat is more intense; by noon you feel that at some point you have inadvertently died and are merely reliving the scene in your head. A rickshaw or taxi never passes through, and you must go on and on until you come out somewhere. Layers of dried betel-spit coat the walls and pavements; it ought to look like dried blood, but it is a little too red. The pervading odour is that of any Chinese grocery store: above all, dried fish, but with strong suggestions of spices and incense. And there are, indeed, a few Chinese here in the Pettah, although most of them appear to be dentists. I remember that one is named Thin Sin Fa, and that he advertizes himself as a "Genuine Chinese Dentist". The mark of their profession is painted over the doorway: a huge red oval enclosing two rows of gleaming white squares. If there is a breeze, pillars of dust sweep majestically through the streets, adding an extra patina of grit to the sweat that covers your skin. In one alley is a poor Hindu temple with a small *gopuram* above the entrance. The hundreds of sculpted figures are not of stone, but of brilliantly painted plaster; banners and pennants hang haphazardly from criss-crossed strings. In another street there is a hideous red brick mosque. The faithful must wear trousers to enter.

There are Hindus and Moslems in every corner of Ceylon, but

neither of these orthodoxies seems fitting for the place. Hinduism is too fanciful and chaotic, Islam too puritanical and austere. Buddhism, with its gentle agnosticism and luxuriant sadness, is so right in Ceylon that you feel it could have been born here, could have grown up out of the soil like the forests. Soon, doubtless, it will no longer be a way of life, having become, along with the rest of the world's religions, a socio-political badge. But for the moment it is still here, still powerful. And in any case, *après nous*, *le déluge*!

ALL PARROTS SPEAK •

Parrots are amusing, decorative, long-lived, and faithful in their affections, but the quality which distinguishes them from most of God's other inventions is their ability to imitate the sounds of human speech. A parrot that cannot talk or sing is, we feel, an incomplete parrot. For some reason it fascinates us to see a small, feather-covered creature with a ludicrous, senile face speaking a human language – so much, indeed, that the more simple-minded of us tend to take seriously the idea suggested by our subconscious: that a parrot really is a person, in disguise, of course, but capable of human thought and feeling.

In Central America and Mexico I have listened for hours while the Indian servants in the kitchen held communion with the parrot – monologues which the occasional interjections from the perch miraculously transformed into conversations. And when I questioned the Indians I found a recurrent theme in their replies: the parrot can be a temporary abode for a human spirit. Our own rational system of thought unhappily forbids such extravagances; nevertheless the atavism is there, felt rather than believed.

The uneducated, unsophisticated Indian, on the other hand, makes an ideal companion and mentor for the parrot. The long colloquies about what to put into the soup, which *rebozo* to wear to the fiesta, are in themselves education of a sort that few of us have the time or patience to provide. It is not surprising that most of the parrots that have found their way to the United States have been trained by rural Latin-Americans. As important as the spoken word in these relationships is a continuous association with one or two individuals. A parrot is not a sociable bird; it usually develops an almost obsessive liking for a very few people, and either indifference or hatred toward everyone else. Its human relationships are simply extentions of its monogamous nature. There is not much difference between being a one-man bird and a one-bird bird.

I remember the day when I first became parrot-conscious.

It was in Costa Rica; Jane and I had been riding all morning with the vaqueros and were very thirsty. At a gatehouse between ranch properties we asked a woman for water. When we had drunk our fill, rested and chatted, she motioned us into a dim corner and said: *"Miren, qué graciosos!"* There, perched on a stick, were seven little creatures. She carried the stick out into the light, and I saw that each of the seven tiny bags of pinkish-grey skin had a perfectly shaped, hooked yellow beak, wide open. And when I looked closely, I could see minature brilliant green feathers growing out of the wrinkles of skin. We discussed the diet and care of young parrots, and our hostess generously offered us one. Jane claimed she couldn't bear to think of breaking up the family, and so we went on our way parrotless.

But a week later, while waiting for a river boat, we had to spend the night in the "hotel" of a hamlet called Bebedero. Our room was built on stilts above a vast mud welter where enormous hogs were wallowing, and it shook perilously when they scratched their backs against the supporting piles. The boat came in fifteen hours late, and there was nothing we could do but sit in the breathlessly hot room and wait. Nothing, that is, until the proprietor appeared in the doorway with a full-grown parrot perched on his finger, and asked us if we wanted to converse with it.

"Does it speak?" I asked.

"Claro que sí. All parrots speak." My ignorance astonished him. Then he added: "Of course it doesn't speak Spanish. Just its own language."

He left it with us. It did indeed speak its own language, something that no philologist would have been able to relate to any dialect. Its favourite word, which it pronounced with the utmost tenderness, was: "Budupple." When it had said that several times with increasing feeling, it would turn its head downward at an eighty-degree angle, add wistfully: "Budupple mah?" and then be quiet for a while.

Of course we bought it; the proprietor put it into a burlap sugar-sack, and we set out downstream with it. The bend of the river just below Bebedero was still visible when it cut its way out of the

24

bag and clambered triumphantly onto my lap. During the rest of the two-day trip to San José the bird was amenable enough if allowed to have its own way unconditionally. In the hotel at San José it ate a lens out of a lorgnette, a tube of tooth paste, and a good part of a Russian novel. Most parrots merely make mincemeat out of things and let the debris fall where it will, but this one actually ate the stuff. We were certain that the glass it had swallowed would bring about a catastrophe, but day after day passed, and Budupple seemed as well as ever. In Puerto Limon we had a cage made for him; unfortunately the only material available was tin, so that by the time we got off the ship at Puerto Barrios and were inside its customhouse the convict had sawed his way through the bars and got out on top of his cage. With his claws firmly grasping the cage roof the bird could lean far out and fasten his beak into whatever presented itself. As we waited in line for the various official tortures to begin, what presented itself was a very stout French lady under whose skirt he poked his head, and up whose fleshy calf he then endeavoured to climb, using beak and claw. It provided an engrossing intermission for the other voyagers.

The next morning, with six porters in tow, we were running through the streets to catch the train for the capital; at one point, when I set the cage down to shift burdens, Budupple slid to the ground and waddled off toward a mango tree. I threw the cage after him and we hurried on to where the train was waiting. We got in; it had just begun to move when there was a commotion on the platform and Budupple was thrust through the open window onto the seat. The Indian who had perpetrated this enormity had just time to say: "*Aqué está su loro*," and wave the battered cage victoriously up and down as a gesture of farewell. Tin is evidently worth more than parrot flesh in Puerto Barrios.

A few days later we arrived in Antigua, where we let Budupple get up into an avocado tree in the back patio of the *pension* and stay. I have often wondered if he managed to survive the resident iguana that regularly took its toll of ducks and chickens.

It might seem that after so inauspicious an introduction to parrot-keeping, I should have been content to live quietly with my memories. But I kept wondering what Budupple would have been like under happier circumstances. After all, a parrot is not supposed to travel continually. And the more I reflected, the more firmly I determined to try another bird. Two years later I found myself in Acapulco with a house whose wooded patio seemed to have ample room for whatever birds or beasts I might wish.

I started out with a Mexican *cotorro*. To a casual observer a *cotorro* looks like a slightly smaller parrot. Its feathers are the same green – perhaps a shade darker – and it has the general characteristics of a parrot, save that the beak is smaller, and the head feathers, which would be yellow on a *loro real* (the Latin Americans' name for what we call a parrot), are orange instead. Neither this *cotorro*, nor any other I ever had, learned to say anything intelligible. If you can imagine a tape-recording of an old-fashioned rubber-bulbed Parisian taxi horn run off at double speed, you have a fair idea of what their conversation sounds like. The only sign of intelligence this *cotorro* displayed was to greet me by blowing his little taxi horn imperiously, over and over. After I had set him free I went out and got a true parrot.

This one came to be the darling of the servants, because, although he had no linguistic repertory to speak of, he could do a sort of Black Bottom on his perch, and sing correctly, imitating the sound of a bugle, a certain military march almost to the end. The kitchen was his headquarters, where, when things got dull for Rosa, Amparo and Antonio, they could bribe him with pieces of banana and tortilla into performing. Occasionally he wandered into the patio or along the *corredor* to visit the rest of the house, but he liked best the dimness and smoke of the kitchen where five minutes seldom passed without his being scratched, or fed, or at least addressed.

The next psittacine annexation to the household (in the interim there came an armadillo, an ocelot and a tejon – a tropical version of the raccoon) was a parakeet named Hitler. He was about four inches high and no one could touch him. All day he strutted about the house scolding, in an eternal rage, sometimes pecking at the servants' bare toes. His voice was a sputter and a squeak, and his Spanish never got any further than the two words *"periquito burro"*, which always came at the end of one of his diatribes, when trembling with emotion, he would pronounce them in a way that recalled the classical orator with his "I have spoken." He was not a very interesting individual because his personality was monochromatic, but I became attached to him: his energy was incredible. When I moved away he was the only member of the menagerie that I took with me.

For some time I had had my eye on a spectacular macaw that lived up the street. She was magnificently red, with blue and yellow trimmings, and she had a voice that could have shouted orders in a foundry. I used to go some afternoons and study her vocal abilities; after a while I decided I wanted her, although I remained convinced that the few recognizable words she was capable of screaming owed their intelligibility solely to chance. It was unlikely that anyone had ever spoken to her of the Oriental dessert known as *baklava*, or of the Battle of Balaklava, and even less probable that she had overheard discussions concerning Max Ernst's surrealist picture book, *La Femme Cent Têtes*, in which the principal character is a monster called Loplop. All three of these words, however, figured prominently in her monologues. Sometimes she threw in the Spanish word *agua*, giving equal and dire stress to each syllable. But I think even that was luck. At all events, soon she was in my patio, driving the entire household, including the other birds, into a frenzy of irritability. At five o'clock every morning she climbed to the top of the lemon tree, the highest point in the neighbourhood, flapped her clipped wings with a sound like bedsheets in the wind, and let loose that unbelievable voice. Nothing could have brought her down, save perhaps the revolver of the policeman who lived three doors away and who came early one morning to the house, weapon in hand, ready to do the deed if he could get into the patio. *"No puedo más, señor,"* he explained. (He went away with two pesos to buy tequila.)

There is a certain lizardlike quality still discernible in the psittacine birds; this is particularly striking in the macaw, the most unlikely and outlandish-looking of the family. Whenever I watched Loplop closely I thought of the giant parrots whose fossils were found not so long ago in Brazil. All macaws have something antediluvian about them. In the open, when they fly in groups, making their peculiar elliptical spirals, they look like any other large bright birds; but when they are reduced by the loss of their wing tips and tail feathers to waddling, crawling, climbing and flopping, they look strangely natural, as if they might have an atavistic memory of a time when they were without those appendages and moved about as they do now in captivity.

The word "captivity" is not really apt, since in Latin America no one keeps macaws in cages; they are always loose, sometimes on perches, or in nearby trees, and it seems never to occur to them to want to escape. The only macaws I have seen chained or caged belonged to Americans; they were vicious and ill-tempered, and the owners announced that fact with a certain pride. The parrot, too, although less fierce in its love of freedom and movement, loathes being incarcerated. It has a fondness for its cage (provided the floor is kept clean) but it wants the door left open so that it can go in and out as it pleases. There is not much point in having a parrot if you are going to keep it caged.

Loplop was headstrong and incurably greedy. She had her own bowl of very sweet *café con leche* in a corner of the floor, and whatever we gave her she dipped into the bowl before devouring it. The edible contributions we made during mealtimes were more like blood money than disinterested gifts, for we would have handed her practically anything on the table to keep her from climbing up there. Once she did that, all was lost. Silverware was scattered, cups were overturned, food flew. She went *through* things; one thought of a snowplow. It was not that we spoiled her, but anyone will reflect a moment before crossing a creature with a beak like a pair of hedge clippers.

The afternoon Jane left for a weekend in Taxco, Loplop decided that I was lonely. She came to tell me so while I was lying in a hammock. Reaching up from the floor and using my posterior for leverage, she climbed into the hammock. I moved quickly to another, taking care first to raise it well into the air. She gurgled. If I wanted to make things difficult, it was quite all right with her: she had the next fifty years or so to achieve her aim. She clambered down, pushed across the floor, shinnied up one of the posts that held the hammock, and slid down the rope into my lap. By the time I realized what had happened, it was too late. I was in my bathing trunks, and she made it quite clear that if I attempted to lift her off she would show no mercy. All she wanted was to have her belly scratched, but she wanted it badly and for an indefinite period of time. For two hours I half-heartedly tickled and scratched her underside, while she lay on her back opening and closing her idiotic eyes, a prey to some mysterious, uncatalogued avian ecstasy. From that day onwards she followed me through the house, ogling me, screaming "Baklava! Loplop!", trying to use my legs as a tree trunk to climb up to my face. Absolute devotion, while admirable, tends to become tedious. I sold Loplop back to the ladies from whom I had brought her.

The following year I found the best of all my Amazons, a perfect *loro real* with a great gift for mimicry. I looked into a little garden, and there it was, perched in its cage, demurely conscious of being stared at. I approached it, said: *"Cómo te llamas?"* and it slowly turned itself upside down before it put its head to the bars nearest me and replied in a coquettish falsetto that was almost a whisper: "Co-to-*rri*-to." This, although it was in truth its name, was obviously a misnomer, for the bird was not a *cotorro* but a parrot, and a large-sized one. We had a short conversation about the weather, after which I bought my new friend, cage and all, for six dollars, and carried it home, to the delight of the Indian maids, who felt that the kitchen was not complete without a *loro* to talk to during the long hours they spent combing their hair. They wanted beauty advice. *"Te gusta así?"* they would say, and then, changing the position of the tresses, comb in mouth, *"O así? Eh, lorito?"*

This bird had star quality. He could not bear to share the stage with any of his fellows. If the *periquito* so much as squeaked, he would silence him with a well-placed shriek. If the *cotorro* just made the customary taxi-horn noise, the parrot started toward it, chuckling evilly, and the *cotorro*, while not too bright, was bright enough to heed the warning. (I found it dead one morning from having cleaned a paintbrush too thoroughly; nothing ever looked deader or more beautifully laid out than that *cotorro* lying on its back with its plump feathered belly facing upward and its two claws curved daintily in rigor mortis. The parrot was unusually energetic and voluble that morning, and I wondered fleetingly if during the night he might not have delivered, for the *cotorro's* benefit, a little discourse on the succulence of wet paint.)

Cotorrito was an intelligent bird – well-balanced emotionally, and with a passion for regularity. He wanted his cage uncovered at half past six in the morning, a banana at seven. About nine he had to be let out, so he could perch on top of his cage, where he would stay until noon. Then he made his tour of inspection of the house, toddling from room to room, just to be sure the place was in order. After that he climbed on to an old bicycle-tyre, hung in a shady part of the patio, and remained perched there while we ate lunch nearby, joining in the conversation with short comments such as *"Verdad?" "Cómo?"* or *"Ay!"* and bursting into hysterical giggles if the talk became more animated than usual. During the afternoon he took his siesta along with the rest of the household. When the shadows lengthened he grew lyrical, as parrots have a way of doing toward the end of the day, and when the maids gathered in the kitchen to prepare dinner he went back there, climbed atop his cage and superintended their work for two hours or so. When he got sleepy, he stepped into the cage and softly demanded to have the door shut and the cover over him.

His performing repertory seemed to be a matter of degree of excitement rather than of choice. Tranquillity expressed itself in a whispered monologue, quite unintelligible, punctuated with short remarks in Spanish. One step above that took him completely into Spanish. From there he went into his giggles, from that into strident song. (He must at some point have lived within hearing of a very bad soprano, because the flatted notes of a song which began *"No sé qué frio extraño se ha metido en mi corazon . . ."* were always identical.) Beyond that there came a strange rural domestic scene which began with a baby that cried, sobbed, and choked for lack of breath, went on to a comforting mother, an effete-sounding father who shouted: "*Cállate!*", a very nervous dog which yapped, and several varieties of poultry including a turkey; and if his emotion exceeded even this stage, which happened very seldom, he let loose a series of jungle calls. Whoever was within hearing quickly departed, in sheer self-protection. Under normal circumstances these different emotional planes were fairly widely separated, but a good loud jazz record could induce a rough synopsis of the entire gamut. The sound of the clarinet above all stimulated him: giggling went into wailing, wailing into barking, barking turned swiftly into jungle calls, and at that point one had to take the record off or leave the house.

Cotorrito was a good parrot: he bit me only once, and that was not his fault. It was in Mexico City. I had bought a pair of new shoes which turned out to be squeaky, and I was wearing them when I came into the apartment after dark. I neglected to turn on the light, and without speaking walked straight to where Cotorrito was perched on top of his cage. He heard the unfamiliar shoes, leaned out, and attacked the stranger. When he discovered his shameful error he pretended it had been due only to extreme sleepiness, but I had roused him from sleep innumerable times with no such deplorable result.

Two parrots live with me now. I put it thus, rather than: "I own two parrots", because there is something about them that makes it very difficult to claim them as one's property. The little person that spends its entire day observing the minutiae of your habits and vocal inflections is more like a rather critical friend who comes for an indefinite stay in your home. Both of my present birds have gone away again at various times; one way or another they have been found, ransomed from their more recent friends, and brought back home. Seth, the African Grey, is the greatest virtuoso performer I have ever had. (But then, African Greys are all geniuses beside Amazons; it is unfair to compare them.) He was born in a suburb of Léopoldville in August, 1955, and thus by parrot standards is still an infant-in-arms. If he continues to study under his present teacher, a devout Moslem lady who works in my kitchen, he ought,

31

like any good Moslem, to know quite a bit of the Koran by the time he reaches adolescence. The other guest, who has been with me for the past fourteen years, is a yellow-headed Amazon. I bought him from a Moroccan who was hawking him around the streets of Tangier, and who insisted his name was Babarhio, which is Moghrebi for parrot. I took him to a blacksmith's to break the chains which fettered his legs. The screams which accompanied this operation drew an enormous crowd; there was great hilarity when he drew blood from the blacksmith's hand. Much more difficult was the task of finding him a cage. There was not one for sale in Tangier strong enough to hold him. I finally heard of an English lady living far out on the Old Mountain whose parrot had died some years ago. Possibly she would still have its cage. During the week it took her to find it, Babarhio made a series of interesting wire sculptures of the two cages I had bought him in the market, and wreaked general havoc in my hotel room. However much freedom one may give a parrot once it has been broken in to its surroundings, it certainly is not feasible at the outset; only chaos can ensue.

Almost immediately I got him used to travelling. I kept him warm by wrapping around the cage two of the long woollen sashes that are worn by the men here, and putting a child's *djellaba* of white wool over everything. The little sleeves stuck out, and the cage looked vaguely like a baby with a large brass ring for a head. It was not a reassuring object, above all when the invisible parrot coughed and chuckled as he often did when he was bored with the darkness of his cage.

There is no denying that in tropical and subtropical countries a parrot makes a most amusing and satisfactory companion about the house, a friend you miss very much when it is no longer with you. Doña Violeta, a middle-aged widow who sold bread in the market of Ocosingo, had hers some thirty years, and when a dog killed it, she was so deeply affected that she closed her stall for three days. Afterwards, when she resumed business, with the embalmed body of her pet lying in state in a small glass-covered coffin on her counter, she was shattered, disconsolate, and burst into tears whenever one showed signs of commiserating with her.

"He was my only friend in the world," she would sob. This of course was quite untrue; one can forgive its exaggeration only by considering her bereavement. But when she added: "He was the only one who understood me," she was coming nearer the truth – a purely subjective one, perhaps, but still a truth. In my mind I have a picture of Doña Violeta in her little room, pouring her heart out to the bird that sat before her attentively, now and then making a senseless remark which she could interpret as she chose. The spoken word, even if devoid of reason, means a great deal to a lonely human being.

I think my susceptibility to parrots may have been partly determined by a story I heard when I was a child. One of the collection of parrots from the New World presented to King Ferdinand by Columbus escaped from the palace into the forest. A peasant saw it, and never having encountered such a bird before, picked up a stone to hit it, so he could have its brilliant feathers as a trophy. As he was taking aim, the parrot cocked its head and cried: "*Ay, Dios!*" Horrified, the man dropped the stone, prostrated himself, and said: "A thousand pardons, *señora*! I thought you were a green bird."

NOTES MAILED AT NAGERCOIL •

I have been here in this hotel now for a week. At no time during the night or day has the temperature been low enough for comfort; it fluctuates between 95 and 105 degrees, and most of the time there is absolutely no breeze, which is astonishing for the seaside. Each bedroom and public room has the regulation large electric fan in its ceiling, but there is no electricity; we are obliged to use oil lamps for lighting. Today at lunchtime a large Cadillac of the latest model drove up to the front door. In the back were three little men wearing nothing but the flimsy dhotis they had draped around their loins. One of them handed a bunch of keys to the chauffeur, who then got out and came into the hotel. Near the front door is the switch box. He opened it, turned on the current with one of the keys, and throughout the hotel the fans began to whir. Then the three little men got out and went into the dining room where they had their lunch. I ate quickly, so as to get upstairs and lie naked on my bed under the fan. It was an unforgettable fifteen minutes. Then the fan stopped, and I heard the visitors driving away. The hotel manager told me later that they were government employees of the State of Travencore, and that only they had a key to the switch box.[1]

Last night I awoke and opened my eyes. There was no moon; it was still dark, but the light of a star was shining into my face through the open window, from a point high above the Arabian Sea. I sat up, and gazed at it. The light it cast seemed as bright as that of the moon in northern countries; coming through the window, it made its rectangle on the opposite wall, broken by the shadow of my silhouetted head. I held up my hand and moved the fingers,

---

[1]Subsequently Travancore and Cochin have merged to make the province of Kerala.

and their shadow too was definite. There were no other stars visible in that part of the sky; this one blinded them all. It was about an hour before daybreak, which comes shortly after six, and there was not a breath of air. On such still nights the waves breaking on the nearby shore sound like great, deep explosions going on at some distant place. There is the boom, which can be felt as well as heard, and which ends with a sharp rattle and hiss, then a long period of complete silence, and finally, when it seems that there will be no more sound, another sudden boom. The crows begin to scream and chatter while the darkness is still complete.

The town, like the others here in the extreme south, gives the impression of being made of dust. Dust and cow-dung lie in the streets, and the huge crows hop ahead of you as you walk along. When a gust of hot wind wanders in from the sandy wastes beyond the town, the brown fans of the palmyra trees swish and bang against each other; they sound like giant sheets of heavy wrapping paper. The small black men walk quickly, the diamonds in their earlobes flashing. Because of their jewels and the gold thread woven into their dhotis, they all look not merely prosperous, but fantastically wealthy. When the women have diamonds, they are likely to wear them in a hole pierced through the wall of one nostril.

The first time I ever saw India I entered it through Dhanushkodi. An analogous procedure in America would be for a foreigner to get his first glimpse of the United States by crossing the Mexican border illegally and coming out into a remote Arizona village. It was God-forsaken, uncomfortable, and a little frightening, Since then I have landed as a bonafide visitor should, in the impressively large and unbeautiful metropolis of Bombay. But I am glad that my first trip did not bring me in contact with any cities. It is better to go to the villages of a strange land before tyring to understand its towns, above all in a complex place like India. Now, after travelling some eight thousand miles around the country, I know approximately as little as I did on my first arrival. However, I've seen a lot of people and places, and at least I have a somewhat more detailed and precise idea of my ignorance than I did in the beginning.

If you have not taken the precaution of reserving a room in advance, you risk having considerable difficulty in finding one when you land in Bombay. There are very few hotels, and the two or three comfortable ones are always full. I hate being committed to a reservation because the element of adventure is thereby destroyed. The only place I was able to get into when I first arrived, therefore, was something less than a first-class establishment. It was all right during the day and the early hours of the evening. At night, however, every square foot of floor space in the dark corridors was occupied by sleepers who had arrived late and brought their own mats with them; the hotel was able in this way to shelter several hundred extra guests each night. Having their hands and feet kicked and trodden on was apparently a familiar enough experience to them for them never to make any audible objection when the inevitable happened.

Here in Cape Comorin, on the other hand, there are many rooms and they are vast, and at the moment I am the only one staying in the hotel.

It was raining. I was on a bus going from Alleppey to Trivandrum, on my way down here. There were two little Indian nuns on the seat in front of mine. I wondered how they stood the heat in their heavy robes. Sitting near the driver was a man with a thick, fierce moustache who distinguished himself from the other passengers by the fact that in addition to his dhoti he also wore a European shirt; its scalloped tail hung down nearly to his knees. With him he had a voluminous collection of magazines and newspapers in both Tamil and English, and even from where I sat I could not help noticing that all this reading matter had been printed in the Soviet Union.

At a certain moment, near one of the myriad villages that lie smothered in the depths of the palm forests there, the motor suddenly ceased to function, and the bus came to a stop. The driver, not exchanging a single glance with his passengers, let his head fall forward and remain resting on the steering wheel in a posture of despair. Expectantly the people waited a little while, and then they began to get down. One of the first out of the bus was the man with the moustache. He said a hearty goodbye to the occupants in general, although he had not been conversing with any of them, and started up the road carrying his umbrella, but not his armful of printed matter. Then I realized that at some point during the past hour, not foreseeing the failure of the motor and the mass departure which it entailed, he had left a paper or magazine on each empty seat – exactly as our American comrades used to do on subway trains three decades ago.

Almost at the moment I made this discovery, the two nuns had risen and were hurriedly collecting the "literature". They climbed down and ran along the road after the man, calling out in English: "Sir, your papers!" He turned, and they handed them to him. Without saying a word, but with an expression of fury on his face, he took the bundle and continued. But it was impossible to tell from the faces of the two nuns when they returned to gather up their belongings whether or not they were conscious of what they had done.

A few minutes later everyone had left the bus and walked to the village – everyone, that is, but the driver and me. I had too much luggage. Then I spoke to him.

"What's the matter with the bus?"

He shrugged his shoulders.

"How am I going to get to Trivandrum?"

He did not know that, either.

"Couldn't you look into the motor?" I pursued. "It sounded like the fan belt. Maybe you could repair it."

This roused him sufficiently from his apathy to make him turn and look at me.

"We have People's Government here in Travancore," he said. "Not allowed touching motor."

"But who *is* going to repair it, then?"

"Tonight making telephone call to Trivandrum. Making report. Tomorrow or other day they sending inspector to examine."

"And then what?"

"Then inspector making report. Then sending repair crew."

"I see."

37

"People's Government," he said again, by way of helping me to understand. "Not like other government."

"No," I said.

As if to make his meaning clearer, he indicated the seat where the man with the large moustache had sat. "That gentleman Communist."

"Oh, really?" (At least, it was all in the open, and the driver was under no misapprehension at to what the term "People's Government" meant.)

"Very powerful man. Member of Parliament from Travancore."

"Is he a good man, though? Do the people like him?"

"Oh, yes, sir. Powerful man."

"But is he *good*?" I insisted.

He laughed, doubtless at my ingenuousness. "Powerful man all rascals," he said.

Just before nightfall a local bus came along, and with the help of several villagers I transferred my luggage to it and continued on my way.

Most of the impressively heavy Communist vote is cast by the Hindus. The Moslems are generally in less dire economic straits, it is true, but in any case, by virtue of their strict religious views, they do not take kindly to any sort of ideological change. (A convert from Islam is unthinkable; apostasy is virtually non-existent.) If even Christianity has retained too much of its pagan décor to be acceptable to the puritanical Moslem mind, one can imagine the loathing inspired in them by the endless proliferations of Hindu religious art with its gods, demons, metamorphoses and avatars. The two religious systems are antipodal. Fortunately the constant association with the mild and tolerant Hindus has made the Moslems of India far more understanding and tractable than their brothers in Islamic countries further west; there is much less actual friction than one might be led to expect.

During breakfast one morning at the Connemara Hotel in Madras the Moslem head waiter told me a story. He was travelling in the Province of Orissa, where in a certain town there was a Hindu temple which was noted for having five hundred cobras on its premises. He decided he would like to see these famous reptiles. When he had got to the town he hired a carriage and went to the temple. At the door he was met by a priest who offered to show him around. And since the Moslem looked prosperous, the priest suggested a donation of five rupees, to be paid in advance.

"Why so much?" asked the visitor.

"To buy eggs for the cobras. You know, we have five hundred of them."

The Moslem gave him the money on condition that the priest let him see the snakes. For an hour his guide dallied in the many courtyards and galleries, pointing out bas-reliefs, idols, pillars and bells. Finally the Moslem reminded him of their understanding.

"Cobras? Ah, yes. But they are dangerous. Perhaps you would rather see them another day?"

This behaviour on the priest's part had delighted him, he recalled, for it had reinforced his suspicions.

"Not at all," he said. "I want to see them now."

Reluctantly the priest led him into a small alcove behind a large stone Krishna, and pointed into a very dark corner.

"Is this the place?" the visitor asked.

"This is the place."

"But where are the snakes?"

In a tiny enclosure were two sad old cobras, "almost dead from hunger," he assured me. But when his eyes had grown used to the dimness he saw that there were hundreds of eggshells scattered around the floor outside the pen..

"You eat a lot of eggs," he told the priest.

The priest merely said: "Here. Take back your five rupees. But if you are asked about our cobras, please be so kind as to say that you saw five hundred of them here in our temple. Is that all right?"

The episode was meant to illustrate the head waiter's thesis, which was that the Hindus are abject in the practice of their religion; this is the opinion held by the Moslems. On the other hand, it must be remembered that the Hindu considers Islam an incomplete doctrine, far from satisfying. He finds its austerity singularly comfortless, and deplores its lack of mystico-philosophical content, an element in which his own creed is so rich.

I was invited to lunch at one of the cinema studios in the suburbs north of Bombay. We ate our curry outdoors; our hostess was the star of the film then in production. She spoke only Marathi; her husband, who was directing the picture, spoke excellent English. During the course of the meal he told how, as a Hindu, he had been forced to leave his job, his home, his car and his bank account in Karachi at the time of partition, when Pakistan came into existence, and emigrate empty-handed to India, where he managed to remake his life. Another visitor to the studio, an Egyptian, was intensely interested in his story. Presently he interrupted to say; "It is unjust, of course."

"Yes," smiled our host.

"What retaliatory measures does your government plan to take against the Moslems left here in India?"

"None whatever, as far as I know."

The Egyptian was genuinely indignant. "But why not?" he demanded. "It is only right that you apply the same principle. You have plenty of Moslems here still to take action against. And I say that, even though I am a Moslem."

The film director looked at him closely. "You say that *because* you are a Moslem," he told him. "But we cannot put ourselves on that level."

The conversation ended on this not entirely friendly note. A moment later packets of betel were passed around. I promptly broke a tooth, withdrew from the company and went some distance away into the garden. While I, in the interests of science, was examining the mouthful of partially chewed betel leaves and areca nut, trying to find the pieces of bicuspid, the Egyptian came up to me, his face a study in scorn.

"They are afraid of the Moslems. That's the real reason," he whispered. Whether he was right or wrong I was neither qualified nor momentarily disposed to say, but it was a classical exposition of the two opposing moral viewpoints – two concepts of behaviour which cannot quickly be reconciled.

Obviously it is a gigantic task to make a nation out of a place like India, what with Hindus, Parsees, Jainists, Jews, Catholics and Protestants, some of whom may speak the arbitrarily imposed national idiom of Hindi, but most of whom are more likely to know Gujarati, Marathi, Bengali, Urdu, Telugu, Tamil, Malayalam or some other tongue instead. One wonders whether any sort of unifying project can ever be undertaken, or, indeed, whether it is even desirable.

When you come to the border between two provinces you often find bars across the road, and you are obliged to undergo a thorough inspection of your luggage. As in the United States, there is a strict contol of the passage of liquor between wet and dry districts, but that is not the extent of the examination.

Sample of conversation at the border on the Mercara-Cannanore highway:

"What is in there?" (Customs officer.)

"Clothing." (Bowles.)

"And in that?"

"Clothing."

"And in all those?"

"Clothing."

"Open all, please."

After eighteen suitcases have been gone through carefully: "My God, man! Close them all. I could charge duty for all of these goods, but you will never be able to do business with these things here anyway. The Moslem men are too clever."

"But I'm not intending to sell my clothes."

"Shut the luggage. It is duty-free, I tell you."

A professor from Raniket in North India arrived at the hotel here the other day, and we spent a good part of the night sitting on the window seat in my room that overlooks the sea, talking about what one always talks about here: India. Among the many questions I put to him was one concerning the reason why so many of the Hindu temples in South India prohibit entry to non-Hindus, and why they have military guards at the entrances. I imagined I knew the answer in advance: fear of Moslem disturbances. Not at all, he said. The principal purpose was to keep out certain Christian missionaries. I expressed disbelief.

"Of course," he insisted. "They come and jeer during our rituals, ridicule our sacred images."

"But even if they were stupid enough to want to do such things," I objected, "their sense of decorum would keep them from behaving like that."

He merely laughed. "Obviously you don't know them."

The post office here is a small stifling room over a shop, and it is full of boys seated on straw mats. The postmaster, a tiny old man who wears large diamond earrings and gold-rimmed spectacles, and is always naked to the waist, is also a professor; he interrupts his academic work to sell an occasional stamp. At first contact his English sounds fluent enough, but soon one discovers that it is not adapted to conversation, and that one can scarcely talk to him. Since the boys are listening, he must pretend to be omniscient, therefore he answers promptly with more or less whatever phrase comes into his head.

Yesterday I went to post a letter by airmail to Tangier. "Tanjore," he said, adjusting his spectacles. "That will be four annas." (Tanjore is in South India, near Trichinopoly.) I explained that I hoped my letter would be going to Tangier, Morocco.

"Yes, yes," he said impatiently. "There are many Tanjores." He opened the book of postal regulations and read aloud from it, quite at random, for (although it may be difficult to believe) exactly six minutes. I stood still, fascinated, and let him go on. Finally he looked up and said: "There is no mention of Tangier. No airplanes go to that place."

"Well, how much would it be to send it by sea mail?" (I thought we could then calculate the sucharge for air mail, but I had misjudged my man.)

"Yes," he replied evenly. "That is a good method, too."

I decided to keep the letter and post it in the nearby town of Nagercoil another day. In a little while I shall have several to add to it, and I count on being able to send them all together when I go. Before I left the post office I hazarded the remark that the weather was extremely hot. In that airless attic at noon it was a wild understatement. But it did not please the postmaster at all. Deliberately he removed his glasses and pointed the stems at me.

"Here we have the perfect climate," he told me. "Neither too cold nor too cool."

"That is true," I said. "Thank you."

In the past few years there have been visible quantitative changes in the life, all in the one direction of Europeanization. This is in the smaller towns; the cities of course have long since been Westernized. The temples which before were lighted by bare electric bulbs and coconut oil lamps now have fluorescent tubes glimmering in their ceilings. Crimson, green, and amber floodlights are used to illumine bathing tanks, deities, the gateways of temples. The public-address system is the bane of the ear these days, even in the temples. And it is impossible to attend a concert or a dance recital without discovering several loudspeakers in operation, whose noise completely destroys the quality of the music. A mile before you arrive at the cinema of a small town you can hear the raucous blaring of the amplifier they have set up at its entrance.

This year in South India there are fewer men with bare torsos, dhotis and sandals: more shirts, trousers and shoes. There is at the same time a slow shutting-down of services which to the Western tourist make all the difference between pleasure and discomfort in travelling, such as the restaurants in the stations (there being no dining-cars on the trains) and the showers in the first-class compartments. A few years ago they worked; now they have been sealed off. You can choke on the dust and soot of your compartment, or drown in your own sweat now, for all the railway cares.

At one point I was held for forty-eight hours in a concentration camp run by the Ceylon government on Indian soil. (The euphemism for this one was "screening camp".) I was told that I was under suspicion of being an "international spy". My astonishment and indignation were regarded as almost convincing in their sincerity, thus proof of my guilt.

"But who am I supposed to be spying *for*?" I asked piteously.

The director shrugged. "Spying for international," he said.

43

More than the insects or the howling of pariah dogs outside the rolls of barbed wire, what bothered me was the fact that in the centre of the camp, which at that time housed some twenty thousand people, there was a loudspeaker in a high tower which during every moment of the day roared forth Indian film music. Fortunately it was silenced at ten o'clock each evening. I got out of the hell-hole by making such violent trouble that I was dragged before the camp doctor, who decided that I was dangerously unbalanced. The idea in letting me go was that I would be detained further along, and the responsibility would fall on other shoulders. "They will hold him at Talaimannar," I heard the doctor say. "The poor fellow is quite mad."

Here and there, in places like the bar of the Hotel Metropole at Mysore, or at the North Coorg Club of Mercara, one may still come across vestiges of the old colonial life; ghosts in the form of incredibly sunburned Englishmen in jodhpurs and boots discussing their hunting luck and prowess. But these visions are exceedingly rare in a land that wants to forget their existence.

The younger generation in India is intent on forgetting a good many things, including some that it might do better to remember. There would seem to be no good reason for getting rid of their country's most ancient heritage, the religion of Hinduism, or of its most recent acquisition, the tradition of independence. This latter, at least insofar as the illiterate masses are concerned, is inseparable not only from the religious state of mind which made political victory possible, but also from the legend which, growing up around the figure of Gandhi, has elevated him in their minds to the status of a god.

The young, politically-minded intellectuals find this not at all to their liking; in their articles and addresses they have returned again and again to the attack against Gandhi as a "betrayer" of the Indian people. That they are motivated by hatred is obvious. But what do they hate?

For one thing, subconsciously they cannot accept their own inability to go on having religious beliefs. Then, belonging to the group without faith, they are thereby forced to hate the past,

44

particularly the atavisms which are made apparent by the workings of the human mind with its irrationality, its subjective involvement in exterior phenomena. The floods of poisonous words they pour forth are directed primarily at the adolescents: it is an age group which is often likely to find demagoguery more attractive than common sense.

There are at least a few of these enlightened adolescents in every town; the ones here in Cape Comorin were horrified when, by a stratagem I led them to the home of a man of their own village named Subramaniam, who claims that his brother is under a spell. (They had not imagined, they told me later, that an American would believe such nonsense.) According to Subramaniam, his brother was a painter who had been made art-director of a major film studio in Madras. To substantiate his story he brought out a sheaf of very professional sketches for film sets.

"Then my brother had angry words with a jealous man in the studio," said Subramaniam, "and the man put a charm on him. His mind is gone. But at the end of the year it will return." The brother presently appeared in the courtyard; he was a vacant-eyed man with a beard, and he had a voluminous turkish towel draped over his head and shoulders. He walked past us and disappeared through a doorway.

"A spirit doctor is treating him . . . " The modern young men shifted their feet miserably; it was unbearable that an American should be witnessing such shameful revelations, and that they should be coming from one in their midst.

But these youths who found it so necessary to ridicule poor Subramaniam failed to understand why I laughed when, the conversation changing to the subject of cows, I watched their collective expression swiftly change to one of respect bordering on beatitude. For cow-worship is one facet of popular Hinduism which has not yet been totally superseded by twentieth-century faithlessness. True, it has taken on new forms of ritual. Mass cow worship is often practised now in vast modern concrete stadiums, with prizes being distributed to the owners of the finest bovine specimens, but the religious aspect of the celebration is still evident. The cows

45

are decorated with garlands and jewellery, fed bananas and sugar-cane by people who have waited in line for hours to be granted that rare privilege, and when the satiated animals can eat no more they simply lie down or wander about, while hundreds of young girls perform sacred dances in their honour.

In India, where the cow wishes to go, she goes. She may be lying in the temple, where she may decide to get up, to go and lie instead in the middle of the street. If she is annoyed by the proximity of the traffic streaming past her, she may lumber to her feet again and continue down the street to the railway station, where, should she feel like reclining in front of the ticket window, no one will disturb her. On the highways she seems to know that the drivers of trucks and buses will spot her a mile away and slow down almost to a stop before they get to her, and that therefore she need not move out from under the shade of the particular banyan tree she has chosen for her rest. Her superior position in the world is agreed upon by common consent.

The most satisfying exposition I have seen of the average Hindu's feeling about this exalted beast is a little essay composed by a candidate for a post in one of the public services, entitled simply: *The Cow*. The fact that it was submitted in order to show the aspirant's mastery of the English language, while touching, is of secondary importance.

The Cow

The cow is one wonderful animal, also he is quadruped and because he is female he gives milk – but he will do so only when he has got child. He is same like God, sacred to Hindu and useful to man. But he has got four legs together. Two are foreward and two are afterwards.

His whole body can be utilized for use. More so the milk. What it cannot do? Various ghee, butter, cream, curds, whey, kova and the condensed milk and so forth. Also, he is useful to cobbler, watermans and mankind generally.

His motion is slow only. That is because he is of amplitudinous species, and also his other motion is much useful to trees, plants as well as making fires. This is done by making flat cakes in hand and drying in the sun.

He is the only animal that extricates his feedings after eating. Then afterwards he eats by his teeth whom are situated in the inside of his mouth. He is incessantly grazing in the meadows.

His only attacking and defending weapons are his horns, especially when he has got child. This is done by bowing his head whereby he causes the weapons to be parallel to ground of earth and instantly proceeds with great velocity forwards.

He has got tail also, but not like other similar animals. It has hairs on the end of the other side. This is done to frighten away the flies which alight on his whole body and chastises him unceasingly, whereupon he gives hit with it.

The palms of his feet are so soft unto the touch, so that the grasses he eats would not get crushed. At night he reposes by going down on the ground and then he shuts his eyes like his relative the horse which does not do so. This is the cow.

The moths and night insects flutter about my single oil lamp. Occasionally, at the top of its chimney, one of them goes up in a swift, bright flame. On the concrete floor in a fairly well-defined ring around the bottom of my chair are the drops of sweat that have rolled off my body during the past two hours. The doors into both the bedroom and the bathroom are shut; I work each night in the dressing-room between them, because fewer insects are attracted here. But the air is nearly unbreathable with the stale smoke of cigarettes and bathi sticks burned to discourage the entry of winged creatures. Today's paper announced an outbreak of bubonic plague in Bellary. I keep thinking about it, and I wonder if the almost certain eventual victory over such diseases will prove to have been worth its price: the extinction of the beliefs and rituals which gave a satisfactory meaning to the period of consciousness that goes between birth and death. I doubt it. Security is a false god; begin making sacrifices to it and you are lost.

A MAN MUST NOT BE VERY MOSLEM •

—Aboard m/s TARSUS,
Turkish Maritime Lines

When I announced my intention of bringing Abdeslam along to
Istanbul, the general opinion of my friends was that there were a
good many more intelligent things to do in the world than to carry
a Moroccan Moslem along with one to Turkey. I don't know. He
may end up as a dead weight, but my hope is that he will turn out
instead to be a kind of pass-key to the place. He knows how to
deal with Moslems, and he has the Moslem sense of seemliness and
protocol. He has also an intuitive gift for the immediate understanding of a situation, and at the same time is completely lacking
in reticence or inhibitions. He can lie so well that he convinces
himself straightway, and he is a master at bargaining: it is a black
day for him when he has to pay the asking price for anything. He
never knows what is printed on a sign because he is totally illiterate;
besides, even if he did know he would pay no attention, for he is
wholly deficient in respect for law. If you mention that this or that
thing is forbidden, he is contemptuous: "Agh! A decree for the
wind!" Obviously he is far better equipped than I to squeeze that
last drop of adventure out of any occasion. I, unfortunately, *can*
read signs, but can't lie or bargain effectively, and will forgo any
joy rather than risk unpleasantness or reprimand from whatever
quarter. At all events, the die is cast: Abdeslam is here on this ship.

My first intimation of Turkey came during tea this afternoon
as the ship was leaving the Bay of Naples. The orchestra was playing
a tango which finally established its identity, after several *reprises*,
as the *Indian Love Call*, and the cliffs of Capri were getting in the
way of the sunset. I glanced at a biscuit that I was about to put
into my mouth, then stopped the operation to examine it more
closely. It was an ordinary little arrowroot tea-biscuit, and on it
were embossed the words HAYD PARK. Contemplating this edible

titbit, I recalled what friends had told me of the amusing havoc that results when the Turks phoneticize words borrowed from other languages. These metamorphosed words have a way of looking like gibberish until you say them aloud, and then more likely than not they resolve themselves into perfectly comprehensible English or French, or even, occasionally, Arabic. SKOC TUID looks like nothing; suddenly it becomes Scotch Tweed. TUALET, TRENCKOT, OTOTEKNIK and SEKSOLOJI likewise reveal their messages as one stares at them. Synthetic orthography is a constantly visible reminder of Turkey's determination to be "modern". The country has turned its back on the East and on Eastern concepts, not with the simple yearning of other Islamic countries to be European or to acquire American techniques, but with a conscious will to transform itself from the core outward, – even to destroy itself culturally, if need be.

—Tarabya, Bosphorus

This afternoon it was blustery and very cold. The water in the tiny Sea of Marmara was choppy and dark, laced with froth; the ship rolled more heavily than it had at any time during its three days out on the open Mediterranean. If the first sight of Istanbul was impressive, it was because the perfect hoop of a rainbow painted across the lead-coloured sky ahead kept one from looking at the depressing array of factory smokestacks along the western shore. After an hour's moving backward and forward in the harbour we were close enough to see the needles of the minarets (and how many of them!) in black against the final flare-up of the sunset. It was a poetic introduction, and like the introductions to most books, it had very little to do with what followed. *Poetic* is not among the adjectives you would use to describe the disembarkation. The pier was festive; it looked like an elegant waterside restaurant or one of the larger Latin-American airports – brilliantly illumined, awnings flapping, its decks mobbed with screaming people.

The customs house was the epitome of confusion for a half hour or so; when eventually an inspector was assigned us, we were

fortunate enough to be let through without having to open anything. The taxis were parked in the dark on the far side of a vast
puddle of water, for it had been raining. I had determined on a
hotel in Istanbul proper, rather than one of those in Beyoglu,
across the Golden Horn, but the taxi-driver and his front-seat
companion were loath to take me there. "All hotels in Beyoglu,"
they insisted. I knew better, and did some insisting of my own.
We shot into the stream of traffic, across the Galata Bridge, to the
hotel of my choosing. Unhappily I had neglected, on the advice of
various friends back in Italy, to reserve a room. There was none
to be had. And so on, from hotel to hotel there in Istanbul, back
across the bridge and up the hill to every establishment in Beyoglu.
Nothing, nothing. There are three international conventions in
progress here, and besides, it is vacation time in Turkey; everything is full. Even the m/s *Tarsus*, from which we just emerged,
as well as another ship in the harbour, has been called into service
tonight to be used as a hotel. By half past ten I accepted the sugges-
tion of being driven twenty-five kilometres up the Bosphorus to
this place, where they had assured me by telephone that they
had space.

"Do you want a room with bath?" they asked.

I said I did.

"We haven't any," they told me.

"Then I want a room without bath."

"We have one." That was that.

Once we had left the city behind and were driving along the
dark road, there was nothing for Abdeslam to do but catechise
the two Turks in front. Obviously they did not impress him as
being up-to-the-mark Moslems, and he started by testing their
knowledge of the Koran. I thought they were replying fairly well,
but he was contemptuous. "They don't know anything," he declared
in Moghrebi. Going into English, he asked them: "How many times
one day you pray?"

They laughed.

"People can sleep in mosque?" he pursued. The driver was busy
navigating the curves in the narrow road, but his companion, who

spoke a special brand of English all his own, spoke for him. "Not slep in mosque many people every got hoss," he explained.

"You make sins?" continued Abdeslam, intent on unearthing the hidden flaws in the behaviour of these foreigners. "Pork, wine?"

The other shrugged his shoulders. "Muslim people every not eat pork not drink wine but maybe one hundred year ago like that. Now different."

"*Never* different!" shouted Abdeslam sternly. "You not good Moslems here. People not happy. You have bad government. Not like Egypt. Egypt have good government. Egypt one-hundred percent Moslem."

The other was indignant. "Everybody happy," he protested. "Happy with Egypt too for religion. But the Egypts sometimes fight with Egypts. Arab fight Arabs. Why? I no like Egypt. I in Egypt. I ask my way. They put me say bakhshish. If you ask in Istanbul, you say go my way, he can bring you, but he no say give bakhshish. Before, few people up, plenty people down. Now, you make your business, I make my business. You take your money, I take my money. Before, *you* take *my* money. You rich with *my* money. Before, Turkey like Egypt with Farouk." He stopped to let all this sink in, but Abdeslam was not interested. "Egypt very good country," he retorted, and there was no more conversation until we got here.

The driver's comrade was describing a fascinating new ideology known as democracy. From the beginning of the colloquy I had my notebook out, scribbling his words in the dark as he spoke them. They express the average uneducated Turk's reaction to the new concept. It was only in 1950 that the first completely democratic elections were held. (Have there been any since?) To Abdeslam, who is a traditionally-minded Moslem, the very idea of democracy is meaningless. It is impossible to explain it to him: he will not listen. If an idea is not explicitly formulated in the Koran, it is wrong; it came either directly from Satan or via the Jews, and there is no need to discuss it further.

This hotel, built at the edge of the lapping Bosphorus, is like a huge wooden box. At the base of the balustrade of the grand staircase leading up from the lobby, one on each side, are two life-sized ladies made of lead and painted with white enamel in the hope of making them look like marble. The dining-room's decorations are of a more recent period – the early 'twenties. There are high murals that look as though the artist had made a study of Boutet de Monvel's fashion drawings of the era; long-necked, low-waisted females in cloches and thigh-length skirts, presumably picnicking on the shores of the Bosphorus.

At dinner we were the only people eating, since it was nearly midnight. Abdeslam took advantage of this excellent opportunity by delivering an impassioned harangue (partly in a mixture of Moghrebi and Standard Arabic and partly in English), with the result that by the end of the meal we had fourteen waiters and busboys crowded around the table listening. Then someone thought of fetching the chef. He arrived glistening with sweat and beaming; he had been brought because he spoke more Arabic than the others, which was still not very much. "Old-fashioned Muslim," explained the headwaiter. Abdeslam immediately put him through the *chehade*, and he came off with flying colours, reciting it word for word along with Abdeslam: "*Achhaddouanlaillahainallah* . . . . " The faces of the younger men expressed unmistakable admiration, as well as pleasure at the approval of the esteemed foreigner, but none of them could perform the chef's feat. Presently the manager of the hotel came in, presumably to see what was going on in the dining-room at this late hour. Abdeslam asked for the bill, and objected when he saw that it was written with Roman characters. "Arabic!" he demanded. "You Muslim? Then bring bill in Arabic." Apologetically the manager explained that writing in Arabic was "dangerous", and had been known on occasion to put the man who did it into jail. To this he added, just to make things quite clear, that any man who veiled his wife also went to jail. "A man must not be *very* Moslem," he said. But Abdeslam had had enough. "I *very very* Moslem," he announced. We left the room.

The big beds stand high off the floor, and haven't enough covers on them. I have spread my topcoat over me: it is cold and I should like to leave the windows shut, but the mingled stenches coming from the combined shower-lavatory behind a low partition in the corner are so powerful that such a course is out of the question. The winds moving down from the Black Sea will blow over me all night. Sometime after we had gone to bed, following a long silence during which I thought he had fallen asleep, Abdeslam called over to me: "That Mustapha Kemal was carrion! He ruined his country. The son of a dog!" Because I was writing, and also because I am not sure exactly where I stand in this philosophical dispute, I said: "You're right. *Allah imsik bekhir*."

—Sirkeci

We are installed at Sirkeci on the Istanbul side, in the hotel I had first wanted. Outside the window is a taxi stand. From early morning onward there is the continuous racket of men's voices shouting and horns being blown in a struggle to keep recently arrived taxis from edging in ahead of those that have been waiting in line. The general prohibition of horn-blowing which is in effect everywhere in the city doesn't seem to apply here. The altercations are bitter, and everyone gets involved in them. Taxi-drivers in Istanbul are something of a race apart. They are the only social group who systematically try to take advantage of the foreign visitor. In the ships, restaurants, cafés, the prices asked of the newcomer are the same as those paid by the inhabitants. (In the bazaars buying is automatically a matter of wrangling; that is understood.) The cab-drivers, however, are more actively acquisitive. For form's sake, their vehicles are equipped with meters, but their method of using them is such that they might better do without them. You get into a cab whose meter registers seventeen liras thirty kurus, ask the man to turn it back to zero and start again; he laughs and does nothing. When you get out it registers eighteen liras eighty kurus. You give him the difference, or one lira and a half. Never! He may want two and a half or three and a half or a good deal more, but he will not settle for what seems equitable according to the meter. Since most tourists pay what they are asked and go on their way, he is not prepared for an argument, and he is likely to let his temper run away with him if you are recalcitrant. There is also the pre-arranged-price system of taking a cab. Here the driver goes as slowly and by as circuitous a route as possible, calling out the general neighbourhood of his destination for all the street to hear, so that he can pick up extra fares en route. He will, unless you assert yourself, allow several people to pile in on top of you until there is literally no room left for you to breathe.

The streets are narrow, crooked and often precipitous, traffic is very heavy, and there are many tramcars and buses. The result is that the taxis go like the wind whenever there is a space of a few yards ahead, rushing to the extreme left to get around obstacles before oncoming traffic reaches them. I am used to Paris and Mexico, both cities of evil repute where taxis are concerned, but I think Istanbul might possibly win first prize for thrill-giving.

One day when we had arranged the price beforehand and our driver, having picked up two extra men, had mercifully put them in front with him, he spied a girl standing on the curb, and slowed down to take her in, too. A policeman saw his manoeuvre and did not approve: one girl with five men seemed too likely to cause a disturbance. He blew his whistle menacingly. The driver, rattled, swerved sharply to the left, to pretend he had never thought of such a thing as stopping to pick up a young lady. There was a crash and we were thrown off the seat. We got out; the last we saw of the driver, he was standing in the middle of the street by his battered car, screaming at the man whom he had hit, and holding up all traffic. Abdeslam took down his licence number, in the hope of persuading me to instigate a lawsuit.

Since the use of the horn is proscribed, taxi-drivers can make their presence known only by reaching out the window and pounding violently on the outside of the door. The scraping of the tramcars and the din of the enormous horse-drawn carts thundering over the cobbled pavements make it difficult to judge just how much the horn interdiction reduces noise. The drivers also have a pretty custom of passing back a packet of cigarettes at the beginning of the journey; this is to soften up the victim for the subsequent kill.

On occasion they sing for you. One morning I was entertained all
the way from Sulemaniye to Taksim with *Jezebel* and *Come On-a
My House*. In such cases the traffic warnings on the side of the car
are done in strict rhythm.

Istanbul is a jolly place; it is hard to find any element of the
sinister about it, notwithstanding all the spy novels for which it
provides such a handsome setting. A few of the older buildings are of
stone; but many more of them are built of wood which looks as
though it had never been painted. The cupolas and minarets rise
above the disorder of the city like huge grey fungi growing out of
a vast pile of ashes. For disorder is the visual keynote of Istanbul.
It is not slovenly – only untidy; not dirty, – merely dingy and
drab. And just as you cannot claim it to be a beautiful city, neither
can you accuse it of being uninteresting. Its steep hills and harbour
views remind you a little of San Francisco; its overcrowded streets
recall Bombay; its transportation facilities evoke Venice, for you
can go to so many places by boat, and the boats are continually
making stops. (It costs threepence to get across to Usküdar in
Asia.) Yet the streets in detail are strangely reminiscent of an
America that has almost disappeared. Again and again I have been
reminded of some New England mill town in the time of my childhood. Or a row of little houses will suggest a back street in Stapleton,
on Staten Island. It is a city whose esthetic is that of the unlikely
and incongruous, a photographer's paradise. There is no native
quarter, or, if you like, it is all native quarter. Beyoglu, site of the
so-called "better" establishments, concerns itself as little with
appearances as do the humbler regions on the other side of the
bridges.

You wander down the hill toward Karaköy. Above the harbour
with its thousands of caïques, rowboats, tugs, freighters, and
ferries, lies a pall of smoke and haze through which you can see the
vague outline of the domes and towers of Aya Sofia, Sultan Ahmet
and Süleyimaniye; but to the left and far above all that there is a
pure region next to the sky where the mountains in Asia glisten with
their snow. As you descend the alleys of steps that lead to the
water's level, there are more and more people around you. In

Karaköy itself just to make progress along the pavement requires the best part of your attention. You would think that all of the city's million and a quarter inhabitants were there, on their way to or from Galata Bridge. By Western European standards it is not a well-dressed crowd. The chaotic sartorial effect achieved by the populace in Istanbul is not necessarily due to poverty, but rather to a divergent conception of the uses to which European garments should be put. The mass is not an ethnically homogeneous one. Faces range in type from Levantine through Slavic to Mongoloid, the last belonging principally to the soldiers from eastern Anatolia. Apart from language there seems to be no one element which they all have in common, not even shabbiness, since there are usually, among the others, a few men and women who do understand how to wear their clothing.

Galata Bridge has two levels, the lower of which is a great dock whence the boats leave to go up the Golden Horn and the Bosphorus, across to the Asiatic suburbs, and down to the islands in the Sea of Marmara. The ferries are there, of all sizes and shapes, clinging to the edge like water-beetles to the side of a floating stick. When you get across to the other side of the bridge there are just as many people and just as much traffic, but the buildings are older and the streets narrower, and you begin to realize that you are, after all, in an oriental city. And if you expect to see anything more than the "points of interest", you are going to have to wander for miles on foot. The character of Istanbul derives from a thousand disparate, non-evident details; only by observing the variations and repetitions of such details can you begin to get an idea of the patterns they form. Thus the importance of wandering. The dust is bad. After a few hours of it I usually have a sore throat. I try to get off the main arteries where the horses and drays clatter by, and stay in the alleyways which are too narrow for anything but foot traffic. These lanes occasionally open up into little squares with rugs hanging on the walls and chairs placed in the shade of the grapevines overhead. A few Turks will be sitting about drinking coffee; the narghilahs bubble. Invariably, if I stop and gaze a moment, someone asks me to have some coffee, eat a few green walnuts, and share his pipe.

An irrational disinclination to become involved keeps me from accepting, but today Abdeslam did accept, only to find to his chagrin that the narghilah contained tobacco, and not kif or hashish as he had expected.

Cannabis sativa and its derivatives are strictly prohibited in Turkey, and the natural correlative of this proscription is that alcohol, far from being frowned upon as it is in other Moslem lands, is freely drunk; being a government monopoly it can be bought at any cigarette counter. This fact is no mere detail: it is of primary social importance, since the psychological effects of the two substances are diametrically opposed to each other. Alcohol blurs the personality by loosening inhibitions. The drinker feels, temporarily at least, a sense of participation. Kif abolishes no inhibitions; on the contrary it reinforces them, pushes the individual further back into the recesses of his own isolated personality, pledging him to contemplation and inaction. It is to be expected that there should be a close relationship between the culture of a given society and the means used by its members to achieve release and euphoria. For Judaism and Christianity the means has always been alcohol; for Islam it has been hashish. The first is dynamic in its effects, the other static. If a nation wishes, however mistakenly, to Westernize itself, first let it give up hashish. The rest will follow, more or less as a matter of course. Conversely, in a Western country, if a whole segment of the population desires, for reasons of protest, (as has happened in the United States) to isolate itself in a radical fashion from the society around it, the quickest and surest way is for it to replace alcohol by cannabis.

—Sirkeci

Today in our wanderings we came upon the old fire tower at the top of the hill behind Süleymaniye, and since there was no sign at the door forbidding entry, we stepped in and began to climb the one hundred and eighty rickety wooden steps of the spiral staircase leading to the top. (Abdeslam counted them.) When we had got almost up, we heard strains of Indian music: a radio up there was tuned in to New Delhi. At the same moment a good deal of water came pouring down upon us through the cracks above. We decided to beat a retreat, but then the boy washing the stairs saw us and insisted that we continue to the top and sit a while. The view up up there was magnificent; there is no better place from which to see the city. A charcoal fire was burning in a brazier, and we had tea and listened to some Anatolian songs which presently came over the air. Outside the many windows the wind blew, and the city below, made quiet by distance, spread itself across the rolling landscape on every side, its roof-tiles pink in the autumn sun.

Later we sought out Pandeli's, a restaurant I had heard about but not yet found. This time we managed to discover it, a delapidated little building squeezed in among harness-shops and wholesale fruit stores. We had *pirinc corba*, *beyendeli kebap*, *barbunya fasulya*, and other good things. In the middle of the meal, probably while chewing on the *taze makarna*, I bit my lip. My annoyance with the pain was not mitigated by hearing Abdeslam remark unsympathetically: "If you'd keep you mouth open when you chew, like everybody else, you wouldn't have accidents like this." Pandeli's is the only native restaurant I have seen which doesn't sport a huge refrigerated showcase packed with food. You are usually led to this and told to choose what you want to eat. In the glare of the fluorescent lighting the food looks pallid and untempting, particularly the meat, which has been hacked into unfamiliar-looking cuts. During your meal there is usually a radio playing ancient jazz; occasionally a Turkish or Syrian number comes up. Although the tea is good, it is not good enough to warrant its being served as though it were nectar, in infinitesimal glasses that can be drained at one gulp. (I often order several at once, and this makes for confusion.) When you ask for water, you are brought a tiny bottle capped with tinfoil. Since it is free of charge, I suspect it of being simple tap-water; perhaps I am unjust.

In the evening we went to the very drab red-light district in Beyoglu, just behind the British Consulate-General. The street was mobbed with men and boys. In the entrance door of each house was a small square opening, rather like those through which one used to be denied access to American speakeasies, and framed in each opening, against the dull yellow light within, was a girl's head.

The Turks are the only Moslems I have seen who seem to have got rid of that curious sentiment, (apparently held by all followers of the True Faith,) of inevitable and hopeless difference between themselves and non-Moslems. Subjectively at least they have managed to bridge the gulf created by their religion, that abyss which isolates Islam from the rest of the world. As a result the visitor feels a specific connection with them which is not the mere one-sided sympathy the well-disposed traveller has for the more basic members of other cultures, but is something desired and felt by them as well. They are touchingly eager to understand and please, – so eager, indeed, that they often neglect to listen carefully, and consequently get things all wrong. Their good-will, however, seldom flags, and in the long run this more than compensates for being given the breakfast you did not order, or being sent in the opposite direction from the one in which you wanted to go. There is, of course, the linguistic barrier. One really needs to know Turkish to live in Istanbul. My ignorance of all Altaic languages is total; in the hotel I suffer. The chances are nineteen in twenty that when I give an order things will go wrong, even when I get hold of the housekeeper who speaks French and who assures me calmly that all the other employees are idiots. The hotel is considered by my guide book to be a "de luxe" establishment, – the highest category. Directly after the "de luxe" listings come the "first class" places, which it describes in its own mysterious rhetoric: "These hotels have somewhat luxury, but are still comfortable with every convenience." Having seen the lobbies of several of the hostelries thus pigeonholed, complete with disembowelled divans and abandoned perambulators, I am very thankful to be here in my de luxe suite, where the telephone is white so that I can see the cockroaches on the instrument before I lift it to my lips. At least the insects are discreet, and die obligingly under a mild blast of DDT. It is fortunate I came here: my two insecticide bombs would never have lasted out a sojourn in a first-class hotel.

Santa Sophia? Aya Sofya now, not a living mosque but a dead one like those of Kairouan which can no longer be used because they have been profaned by the feet of infidels. Greek newspapers have carried on propaganda compaigns designed to turn the clock back, reinstate Aya Sofya as a tabernacle of the Orthodox Church. The move was obviously foredoomed to failure: after having used it as a mosque for five centuries the Moslems would scarcely relish seeing it put back into the hands of the Christians. And so now it is a museum which contains nothing but its own architecture. Sultan Ahmet, the mosque just across the park, is more to my own taste, but then, a corpse does not bear comparison to a living organism. Sultan Ahmet is still a place of worship, the *imam* is allowed to wear the classical headgear, the heavy final syllable of Allah's name reverberates in the air under the high dome, boys *doven* in distant corners as they memorize *surat* from the Koran. When the tourists stumble over the prostrate forms of men in prayer, or blatantly make use of their light-meters and Rolleiflexes, no one pays any attention. To Abdeslam this incredible invasion of privacy was tantamount to lack of respect for Islam; it fanned the coals of his resentment into flame. (In his country no unbeliever can put even one foot into a mosque.) As he wandered about, his exclamations of indignation became increasingly audible. He started out with the boys by suggesting to them that it was their great misfortune to be living in a country of widespread sin. They looked at him blankly, and went on with their litanies. Then in a louder voice he began to criticize the raiment of the worshippers, because they wore socks and slippers on their feet, and on their heads berets or caps with the visors at the back. He knows that the wearing of the tarbouche is forbidden by law, but his hatred of Kemal Ataturk, which has been growing hourly ever since his arrival, had become too intense, I suppose, for him to be able to repress it any longer. His big moment came when the *imam* entered. He approached the venerable gentleman with elaborate salaams which were enthusiastically reciprocated. Then the two retired into a private room, where they remained for ten minutes or so. When Abdeslam came out there were tears in his eyes and he wore an expression of triumph. "Ah, you see?" he cried, as we emerged into the street. "That poor man is very, *very* unhappy. They have only one day of Ramadan in the year." (Even I was a little shocked to hear that the traditional month had been whittled down to a day.) "This is an accursed land," he went on. "When we get power we'll soak it in petrol and set it afire, and burn everyone in it. May it forever be damned! And all these dogs living in it, I pray Allah they may be thrown into the fires of Gehennem. Ah, if we only had our power back for one day, we Moslems! May Allah speed that day when we shall ride into Turkey and smash their government and all their works of Satan!" The *imam*, it seems, had been delighted beyond measure to see a young man who still had the proper respect for religion; he had complained bitterly that the youth of Turkey was spiritually lost.

Today I had lunch with a woman who has lived here a good many years. As a Westerner, she felt that the important thing to notice about Turkey is the fact that from having been in the grip of a ruthless dictatorship it has slowly evolved into a modern democracy, rather than having followed the more usual reverse process. Even Ataturk was restrained by his associates from going all the way in his iconoclasm, for what he wanted was a Turkish adaptation of what he had seen happen in Russia. Religion was to him just as much of an opiate in one country as in another. He managed to deal it a critical blow here, one which may yet prove to have been fatal. Last year an American, a member of Jehovah's Witnesses, arrived, and as is the custom with members of that sect, stood on the street handing out brochures. But not for long. The police came, arrested him, put him in jail, and eventually effected his expulsion from the country. This action, insisted my lunch partner, was not taken because the American was distributing Christian propaganda; had he been distributing leaflets advocating the reading of the Koran, it is likely that his punishment would have been more severe.

—Sirkeci

At the beginning of the Sixteenth Century Selim the Grim captured from the Shah of Persia one of the most fantastic pieces of furniture I have ever seen. The trophy was the poor Shah's throne, a simple but massive thing made of chiselled gold, decorated with hundreds of enormous emeralds. I went to see it today at the Topkapi Palace. There was a bed to match, also of emerald-studded gold. After a moment of looking, Abdeslam ran out of the room where these incredible objects stood, into the courtyard, and could not be coaxed back in. "Too many riches are bad for the eyes," he explained. I could not agree; I thought them beautiful. I tried to make him tell me the exact reason for his sudden flight, but he found it difficult to give me a rational explanation of his behaviour. "You know that gold and jewels are sinful," he began. To get him to go on, I said I knew. "And if you look at sinful things for very long you can go crazy; you know that. And I don't want to go crazy." I was willing to take the chance, I replied, and I went back in to see more.

—Sirkeci

These last few days I have spent entirely at the covered souks. I discovered the place purely by accident, since I follow no plan in my wanderings about the city. You climb up an endless hill; whichever street you take swarms with buyers and sellers who take up all the room between the shops on either side. It isn't good form to step on the merchandise, but now and then one can't avoid doing it.

The souks are all in one vast ant-hill of a building, a city within a city, whose avenues and streets, some wide, some narrow, are like the twisting hallways one remembers from a dream. There are more than five thousand shops under its roof, so they assure me; — I have not wondered whether it seems a likely number or not, nor have I passed through all its forty-two entrance portals, nor explored more than a small number of its tunnelled galleries. Visually the individual shops lack the colour and life of the kissarias of Fez and Marrakech, and there are no painted Carthaginian columns like those which decorate the souks in Tunis. The charm of the edifice lies in it svastness, and in part precisely in its dimness and clutter. In the middle of one open space where two large corridors meet, there is an outlandish construction, in shape and size not unlike one of the old traffic towers on New York's Fifth Avenue in the 'twenties. On the ground floor is a minute kitchen. If you climb the crooked outside staircase, you find yourself in a tiny restaurant with four miniature tables. Here you sit and eat, looking out along the tunnels over the heads of the passers-by. It is a place out of Kafka's *Amerika*.

The antique shops here in the souks are famous. As one might expect, tourists are considered to be a feeble-minded and nearly defenseless species of prey, and there are never enough of them to go around. Along the sides of the galleries stand whole tribes of merchants waiting for them to appear. These men have brothers, fathers, uncles and cousins, each of whom operates his own shop, and the tourist is passed along from one member of the family to the next with no visible regret on anyone's part. In ons shop I heard the bearded proprietor solemnly assuring a credulous American woman that the amber perfume she had just bought was obtained by pressing beads of amber like those in the necklace she was examining. (Not that it would have been much more truthful of him had he told her that it was made of ambergris: the amber I have smelled here never saw a whale, and consists almost entirely, I should say, of benzoin.)

If you stop to look into an antiquary's window you are lost. Suddenly you are aware that hands are clutching your clothing, pulling you gently toward the door, and honeyed voices are experimenting with greetings in all the more common European languages, one after the other. Unless you offer physical resistance you find yourself being propelled forcibly within. Then as you face your captors over arrays of old silver and silk, they begin to work on you in earnest, using all the classic clichés of Eastern sales-patter.

"You have such a fine face that I want my merchandise to go with you." "We need money today; you are the first customer to come in all day long." A fat hand taps the ashes from a cigarette. "Unless I do business with you, I won't sleep tonight. I am an old man. Will you ruin my health?" "Just buy one thing, no matter what. Buy the cheapest thing in the store, if you like, but buy something . . . ." If you get out of the place without making a purchase, you are entitled to add ten to your score. A knowledge of Turkish is not necessary here in the bazaars. If you prefer not to speak English or French or German, you find that the Moslems love to be spoken to in Arabic, while the Jews speak a corrupt Andalucîan version of Spanish.

Today I went out of the covered souks by a back street that I had not found before. It led downward toward the Rustempasa Mosque. The shops gave it a strange air: they all looked alike from the outside. On closer inspection I saw that they were all selling the same wildly varied assortment of unlikely objects. I wanted to get in and examine the merchandise, and since Abdeslam had been talking about buying some rubber-soled shoes, we chose a place at random and went into it. While he tried on sneakers and sandals I made a partial inventory of the objects in the big gloomy room. The shelves and counters exhibited footballs, Moslem rosaries, military belts, reed mouthpieces for native oboes, doorhooks, dice of many sizes and colours, narghilahs, watchstraps of false cobra-skin, garden shears, slippers of untanned leather – hard as stone, brass water-taps for kitchen sinks, imitation ivory cigarette-holders ten inches long, suitcases made of pressed paper, tambourines, saddles, assorted medals for the military, and plastic game counters. Hanging from the ceiling were revolver holsters, lutes, and zipper fasteners that looked like strips of flypaper. Ladders were stacked upright against the wall, and on the floor were striped canvas deckchairs, huge tin trunks with scenes of Mecca stamped on their sides, and a great pile of wood-shavings among whose comfortable hills nestled six very bourgeois cats. Abdeslam bought no shoes, and the proprietor began to stare at me and my notebook with unconcealed suspicion, having decided, perhaps, that I was a member of the secret police looking for stolen goods.

A MAN MUST NOT BE VERY MOSLEM

—Sirkeci

Material benefits may be accrued in the process of destroying the meaning of life. Are these benefits worth the inevitable void produced by that destruction? The question is apposite in every case where the traditional beliefs of a people have been systematically modified by its government. Rationalizing words like "progress", "modernization", or "democracy" mean nothing because, even if they are used sincerely, the imposition of such concepts by force from above cancels whatever value they might otherwise have. There is little doubt that by having been made indifferent Moslems the younger generation in Turkey has become more like our idea of what people living in the Twentieth Century should be. The old helplessness in the face of *mektoub* (it is written) is gone, and in its place is a passionate belief in man's ability to alter his destiny. That is the greatest step of all; once it has been made, anything, unfortunately, can happen.

Abdeslam is not a happy person. He sees his world, which he knows is a good world, being assailed from all sides, slowly crumbling before his eyes. He has no means of understanding me, should I try to explain to him that in this age what he considers to be religion is called superstition, and that religion today has come to be a desperate attempt to integrate metaphysics with science. Something will have to be found to replace the basic wisdom which has been destroyed, but the discovery will not be soon; neither Abdeslam nor I will ever know of it.

It had taken the truck fourteen hours to get from Kerzaz to Adrar, and except for the lunch stop in the oasis of El Aougherout, the old man had sat the whole time on the floor without moving, his legs tucked up beneath him, the hood of his burmous pulled up over his turban to protect his face from the fine dust that sifted up through the floor. First-class passage on the vehicles of the Compagnie Générale Transsaharienne entitled the voyager to travel in the glassed-in compartment with the driver, and that was where I sat, occasionally turning to look through the smeared panes at the solitary figure sitting sedately in the midst of the tornado of dust behind. At lunchtime, when I had seen his face with its burning brown eyes and magnificent white beard, it had occurred to me that he looked like a handsome and very serious Santa Claus.

The dust grew worse during the afternoon, so that by sunset, when we finally pulled into Adrar, even the driver and I were covered. I got out and shook myself, and the little old man clambered out of the back, cascades of dust spilling from his garments. Then he came around to the front of the truck to speak to the driver, who, being a good Moslem, wanted to get a shower and wash himself. Unfortunately he was a city Moslem as well as being a good one, so that he was impatient with the measured cadence of his country-man's speech, and slammed the door in middle of it, unaware that the old man's hand was in the way.

Calmly the old man opened the door with his other hand. The tip of his middle finger dangled by a bit of skin. He looked at it an instant, then quietly scooped up a handful of that ubiquitous dust, put the two parts of the finger together and poured the dust over it, saying softly: "Thanks be to Allah." With that, the expression on his face never having changed, he picked up his bundle and staff and walked away. I stood looking after him, full of wonder, and reflecting upon the differences between his behaviour and what mine would have been under the same circumstances. To show no outward sign of pain is unusual enough, but to express no resentment against the person who has hurt you seems very strange, and to give thanks to God at such a moment is the strangest touch of all.

Clearly, examples of such stoical behaviour are not met with every day, or I should not have remembered this one; my experience since then, however, has shown me that it is not untypical, and it has remained with me and become a symbol of that which is admirable in the people of North Africa. "This world we see is unimportant and ephemeral as a dream," they say. "To take it seriously would be an absurdity. Let us think rather of the heavens that surround us." And the landscape is conducive to reflections upon the nature of the infinite. In other parts of Africa you are aware of the earth beneath your feet, of the vegetation and the animals; all power seems concentrated in the earth. In North Africa the earth becomes the less important part of the landscape because you find yourself constantly raising your eyes to look at the sky. In the arid landscape the sky is the final arbiter. When you have understood that, not intellectually but emotionally, you have also understood why it is that the great trinity of monotheistic religions, Judaism, Christianity and Islam, which removed the source of power from the earth itself to the spaces outside the earth, were evolved in desert regions. And of the three, Islam, perhaps because it is the most recent, operates the most directly and with the greatest strength upon the daily actions of those who embrace it.

For a person born into a culture where religion has long ago become a thing quite separate from daily life, it is a startling experience to find himself suddenly in the midst of a culture where there is a minimum of discrepancy between dogma and natural behaviour, and this is one of the great fascinations of being in North Africa. I am not speaking of Egypt, where the old harmony is gone, decayed from within. My own impressions of Egypt before Nasser are those of a great panorama of sun-dried disintegration. In any case, she has had a different history from the rest of Mediterranean Africa; she is ethnically and linguistically distinct, and is more a part of the Levant than of the region we ordinarily mean when we speak of North Africa. But in Tunisia, Algeria and Morocco there are still people whose lives proceed according to the ancient pattern of concord between God and man, agreement between theory and practice, identity of word and flesh (or however one prefers to conceive and define that pristine state of existence we intuitively feel we once enjoyed and now have lost.)

I do not claim that the Moslems of North Africa are a group of mystics, heedless of bodily comfort, interested only in the welfare of the spirit. If you have ever bought so much as an egg from one of them, you have learned that they are quite able to fend for themselves when it comes to money matters. The spoiled strawberries are at the bottom of the basket, the pebbles inextricably mixed with the lentils and the water with the milk, the same as in many other parts of the world, with the difference that if you ask the price of an object in a rural market, they will reply, all in one breath: "Fifty, how much will you give?" I should say that in the realm of *beah o chra* (selling and buying; note that in their minds selling comes first), which is what they call business, they are surpassed only by the Hindus, who are less emotional about it and therefore more successful, and by the Chinese, acknowledged masters of the Oriental branch of the science of commerce.

In Morocco you go into a bazaar to buy a wallet, somehow find yourself being propelled toward the back room to look at antique brass and rugs, are presently seated with a glass of mint tea in your hand and a platter of pastries in your lap, while smiling gentlemen modelling ancient caftans and marriage robes parade in front of you, the salesman who greeted you at the door having completely vanished. Later on you may once again ask timidly to see the wallets, which you noticed on display near the entrance. Likely as not, you will be told that the man in charge of wallets is at the moment saying his prayers, but that he will soon be back, and in the means time would you not be pleased to see some magnificent jewellery from the court of Moulay Ismail? Business is business and prayer-are prayers, and both are a part of the day's work.

When I meet fellow Americans travelling about here in North Africa, I ask them: "What did you expect to find here?" Almost without exception, regardless of the way they express it, the answer, reduced to its simplest terms, is: a sense of mystery. They expect mystery, and they find it, since fortunately it is a quality difficult to extinguish all in a moment. They find it in the patterns of sunlight filtering through the latticework that covers the souks, in the unexpected turnings and tunnels of the narrow streets, in the women whose features still go hidden beneath the litham, in the secretiveness of the architecture, which is such that even if the front door of a house is open, it is impossible to see inside. If they listen as well as look, they find it too in the song the lone camel driver sings by his fire before dawn, in the calling of the muezzins at night, when their voices are like bright beams of sound piercing the silence, and, most often, in the dry beat of the darbouka, the hand drum played by the women everywhere, in the great city houses and in the humblest country hut.

It is a strange sensation, when you are walking alone in a still, dark street late at night, to come upon a pile of carboard boxes soaked with rain, and, as you pass by it, to find yourself staring into the eyes of a man sitting upright behind it. A thief? A beggar? The night watchman of the quarter? A spy for the Secret Police?

You just keep walking, looking at the ground, hearing your footsteps echo between the walls of the deserted street. Into your head comes the idea that you may suddenly hear the sound of a conspiratorial whistle, and that something unpleasant may be about to happen. A little farther along you see, deep in the recess of an arcade of shops, another man reclining in a deck chair, asleep. Then you realize that all along the street there are men both sleeping and sitting quietly awake, and that even in the hours of its most intense silence the place is never empty of people.

It is only since the end of 1955 that Morocco has had its independence, but already there is a nucleus of younger Moslems who fraternize freely with the writers and painters (most of whom are American girls and youths) who have wandered into this part of the world and found it to their liking. Together they give very staid, quiet parties which show a curious blend of Eastern and Western etiquette. Usually no Moslem girls are present. Everyone will be either stretched out on mattresses or seated on the floor, and kif and hashish will be on hand, but half the foreigners will content themselves with highballs. A good many paintings are looked at, and there is a lot of uninformed conversation about art and expression and religion. When food is passed around, the Moslems, for all their passionate devotion to European manners, not only adhere to their own custom of using chunks of bread to sop up the oily *mruq* at the bottom of their plates, but manage to impose the system on the others as well, so that everybody is busy rubbing pieces of bread over his plate. Why not? The food is cooked to be eaten in that fashion, and is less tasty if eaten in any other way.

Many of the Moslems paint, too; after so many centuries of religious taboo with regard to the making of representational images, abstraction is their natural mode of expression. You can see in their canvases the elaboration of design worked out by the Berbers in their crafts: patterns that show constant avoidance of representation but manage all the same to suggest recognizable things. Naturally, their paintings are a great success with the visiting artists, who carry their admiration to the point of imitation. The beat-generation North Africans are music-mad, but they get their music via radio, phonograph and tape-recorder. They are enthusiastic about the music of their own country, but unlike their fathers, they don't sing or play it, because the age of specialization has arrived here too. They are also fond of such exotic items as Congo drumming, the music of India, and particularly the more recent American jazz (Art Blakey, Horace Silver, Cannonball Adderley).

At the moment, writing about any part of Africa is a little like trying to draw a picture of a roller coaster in motion. You can say: it *was* thus and so, or, it *is becoming* this or that, but you risk making a misstatement if you say categorically that anything *is*, because likely as not you will open tomorrow's newspaper to discover that it has changed. On the whole the new governments of Tunisia and Morocco are desirous of furthering tourism in their respective countries; they are learning that the average tourist is more interested in native dancing than in the new bus terminal, that he is more willing to spend money in the Casbah than to inspect new housing projects. For a while, after the demise of the violently unpopular

Pacha of Marrakech, Thami el Glaoui, the great public square of Marrakech, the Djemaa el Fna, was used solely as a parking lot. Anyone will tell you that the biggest single attraction for tourists in all North Africa was the Djemaa el Fna in Marrakech. It was hard to find a moment of the day or night when tourists could not be found prowling around among its acrobats, singers, storytellers, snake charmers, dancers and medicine men. Without it Marrakech became just another Moroccan city. And so the Djemaa el Fna was reinstated, and now goes on more or less as before.

It is clear that the immediate political prospects for Barbary depend in large measure upon what kind of government is established in Algeria, and whether continuing economic ties with France will prove capable of maintaining sufficient prosperity to keep the present pre-democratic regimes of Tunisia and Morocco functioning. Those who want to see the neutralist bloc extended to the Atlantic coast argue that such a development is inevitable since the countries are Moslem and adhere to the Arab League. But North Africa is inhabited, like Malaya and Pakistan, by Moslems who are not Arabs. *Encyclopaedia Britannica's* estimate of the percentage of Arab stock in the population of Morocco dates from two decades ago, but there has been no influx of Arabs since, so we can accept its figure of ten percent as being still valid. The remaining ninety percent of the people are Berbers, who anthropologically have nothing to do with the Arabs. They are not of Semitic origin, and were right where they are now long before the Arab conquerors ever suspected their existence.

Even after thirteen hundred years, the Berbers' conception of how to observe the Moslem religion is by no means identical with that of the descendants of the men who brought it to them. And, the city Moslems complain, they do not observe the fast of Ramadan properly, they neither veil nor segregate their women, and most objectionable of all, they have a passion for forming cults dedicated to the worship of local saints. In this their religious practices show a serious deviation from orthodoxy, inasmuch as during the *moussems*, the gigantic pilgrimages which are held periodically at the many shrines where these holy men are buried, men and women can be seen dancing *together*, working themselves into a prolonged frenzy. This is the height of immorality, the young puritans tell you. Nor is it the extent, they add, of the Berbers' reprehensible behaviour at these manifestations. Self-torture, the inducing of trances, ordeal by fire and the sword, and the eating of broken glass and scorpions are also not unusual on such occasions.

The traveller who has been present at one of these indescribable gatherings will never forget it, although if he dislikes the sight of blood and physical suffering he may try hard to put it out of his mind. To me these spectacles are filled with great beauty, because their obvious purpose is to prove the power of the spirit over the flesh. The sight of ten or twenty thousand people actively declaring their faith, demonstrating *en masse* the power of that faith, can scarcely be anything but inspiring. You lie in the fire, I gash my legs and arms with a knife, he pounds a sharpened bone into his thigh with a rock – then, together, covered with ashes and blood, we sing and dance in joyous praise of the saint and the god who make it possible for us to triumph over pain, and by extension, over death itself. For the participants exhaustion and ecstasy are inseparable.

This cult-worship, based on vestiges of an earlier religion, has long been frowned upon by the devout urban Moslems; as early as the mid-thirties various restrictions were placed on its practice. For a time, public manifestations of it were effectively suppressed. There were several reasons why the educated Moslems objected to the brotherhoods. During the periods of the protectorates in Tunisia and Morocco, the colonial administrations did not hesitate to use them for their own political ends, to ensure more complete domination. Also, it has always been felt that visitors who happened to witness the members of a cult in action were given an unfortunate impression of cultural backwardness. Most important was the fact that the rituals were unorthodox and thus unacceptable to true Moslems. If you mentioned such cults as the Derqaoua, the Aissaoua, the Haddaoua, the Hamatcha, the Jilala or the Guennaoua to a city man, he cried: "They're all criminals! They should be put in jail!" without stopping to reflect that it would be difficult to incarcerate more than half the population of any country. I think one reason why the city folk are so violent in their denunciation of the cults is that most of them are only one generation removed from connection with them themselves; knowing the official attitude toward such things, they feel a certain guilt at being even that much involved with them. Having been born into a family of adepts is not a circumstance which anyone can quickly forget. Each brotherhood has its own songs and drum rhythms, immediately recognizable as such by persons both within and outside the group. In early childhood rhythmical patterns and sequences of tones become a part of an adept's subconscious, and in later life it is not difficult to attain the trance state when one hears them again.

A variation on this phenomenon is the story of Farid. Not long ago he called by to see me. I made tea, and since there was a fire in the fireplace, I took some embers out and put them into a brazier. Over them I sprinkled some *mska*, a translucent yellow resin which makes a sweet, clean-smelling smoke. Moroccans appreciate pleasant odours; Farid is no exception. A little latter, before the embers had cooled off, I added some *djaoui*, a compound resinous substance of uncertain ingredients.

Farid jumped up. "What have you put into the *mijmah*?" he cried.

As soon as I had pronounced the word *djaoui*, he ran into the next room and slammed the door. "Let air into the room!" he shouted. "I can't smell *djaoui*! It's very bad for me!"

When all trace of the scent released by the *djaoui* was gone from the room, I opened the door and Farid came back in, still looking fearful.

"What's the matter with you?" I asked him. "What makes you think a little *djaoui* could hurt you? I've smelled it a hundred times and it's never done me any harm."

He snorted. "You! Of course it couldn't hurt *you*. You're not a *Jilali*, but I am. I don't want to be, but I still am. Last year I hurt myself and had to go to the clinic, all because of *djaoui*."

He had been walking in a street of Emsallah and had stopped in front of a café to talk to a friend. Without warning he had collapsed on the pavement; when he came to, he was at home and a drum was being beaten over him. Then he recalled the smoke that had been issuing from the café, and knew what had happened.

Farid had passed his childhood in a mountain village where all the members of his family were practising Jilala. His earliest memories were of being strapped to his mother's back while she, dancing with the others, attained a state of trance. The two indispensable exterior agents they always used to assure the desired alteration of consciousness were drums and djaoui. By the time the boy was four or five years old, he already had a built-in mechanism, an infallible guarantee of being able to reach the trance state very swiftly in the presence of the proper stimulus. When he moved to the city he ceased to be an adept, and in fact abandoned all religious practice. The conditioned reflex remained, as might be expected, with the result that now as a man in his mid-twenties, although he is at liberty to accept or refuse the effect of the specific drum rhythms, he is entirely at the mercy of a pinch of burning *djaoui*.

His exposition of the therapeutic process by which he is "brought back", each time there is an accident, involves a good many other details, such as the necessity for a member of the paternal side of his family to eat a piece of the offending *djaoui* in his presence, the pronouncing of certain key phrases, and the playing of the proper rhythm on the *bendir* necessary to break the spell. But the indisputable fact remains that when Farid breathes in *djaoui* smoke, whether or not he is aware of doing so, straightway he loses consciousness.

One of my acquaintances who has always been vociferous in his condemnation of the brotherhoods, eventually admitted to me that all the older members of his family were adherents to the *Jilala* cult, citing immediately afterward, as an example of their perniciousness, an experience of his grandmother some three years before. Like the rest of the family, she was brought up as a Jilalía, but had grown too old to take part in the observances, which nowadays are held secretly. (Prohibition, as usual, does not mean abolition, but merely being driven underground.) One evening the old lady was alone in the house, her children and grandchildren having

74

all gone to the cinema, and since she had nothing else to do, she went to bed. Somewhere nearby, on the outskirts of town, there was a meeting of Jilala going on. In her sleep she rose, and, dressed just as she was, began to make her way toward the sounds. She was found next morning unconscious in a vegetable garden near the house where the meeting had taken place, having fallen into an ant colony and been badly stung. The reason she fell, the family assured me, was that at a certain moment the drumming had stopped; it if had gone on she would have arrived. The drummers always continue until everyone present has been brought out of his trance.

"But they did not know she was coming," they said, "and so the next morning, after we had carried her home, we had to send for the drummers to bring her to her senses." It is the sort of story which infuriates the younger generation of French-educated Moslems if they hear it being told to foreigners. And for the latter to be interested in such things upsets them even more. "Are all the people in your country Holy Rollers?" they demand. "Why don't you write about the civilized people here, instead of the most backward?"

I suppose it is natural for them to want to see themselves presented to the outside world in the most "advanced" light possible. They find it perverse of a Westerner to be interested only in the dissimilarities between their culture and his. However, that's the way some of us Westerners are.

Not long ago I wrote on the character of the North Africa Moslem. An illiterate Moroccan friend wanted to know what was in it, and so, in a running translation into Moghrebi, I read him certain passages. His comment was terse: "That's shameful."

"Why?" I demanded.

"Because you've written about people just as they are."

"For us that's not shameful."

"For us it is. You've made us like animals. You've said that only a few of us can read or write."

"Isn't that true?"

"Of course not! We can all read and write, just like you. And we would, if only we'd had lessons."

I thought this interesting and told it to a Moslem lawyer, assuming it would amuse him. It did not. "He's quite right," he announced. "Truth is not what you perceive with your senses, but what you feel in your heart."

"But there is such a thing as objective truth!" I cried. "Or don't you attach importance to that?"

He smiled tolerantly. "Not in the way you do, for its own sake. That is statistical truth. We are interested in that, yes, but only as a means of getting to the real truth underneath. For us there is very little visible truth in the world these days." However specious this kind of talk may seem, it is still clear to me that the lawyer was voicing a feeling common to the great mass of city dwellers here, educated or not.

With an estimated adult illiteracy rate of 80 to 90 percent, perhaps the greatest need of all for North Africa is universal education. So far there has been a very small amount, and as we ourselves say, a little learning is a dangerous thing. The Europeans always have been guilty of massive neglect with regard to schools for Moslems in their North African possessions. In time, their short-sighted policy is likely to prove the heaviest handicap of all in the desperate attempt of the present rulers to keep the region within the Western sphere of influence. The task of educating these people is not made easier by the fact that Moghrebi, the language of the majority, is purely a spoken tongue, and that for reading and writing they must resort to Standard Arabic, which is as far from their idiom as Latin is from Italian. But slowly the transition is taking place. If you sit in a Moroccan café at the hour of a news broadcast, the boy fanning the fire will pause with bellows in his hand, the card players lay down their cards, the talkers cease to argue as the announcer begins to speak, and an expression of ferocious intensity appears on every countenance. Certainly they are vitally interested in what is being said (even the women have taken up the discussion of politics lately), for they are aware of their own increasing importance in the world pattern, but the almost painful expressions are due to each man's effort to understand the words of Standard Arabic as they come over the air. Afterward, there is often an argument as to exactly what the news contained.

"The British are at war with Yemen for being friendly to Gamal Abd el Nasser."

"You're crazy. He said Gamal Abd el Nasser is making war against Yemen because the British are there."

"No. He said Gamal Abd el Nasser *will* make war against Yemen if they let the British in."

"No, no! Against the *British* if they send guns to Yemen."

This state of affairs, if it does not keep all members of the populace accurately informed, at least has the advantage of increasing their familiarity with the language their children are learning at school.

There is a word which non-Moslems invariably use to describe Moslems in general: fanatical. As though the word could not be applied equally well to any group of people who care deeply about anything! Just now, the North African Moslems are passionately involved in proving to themselves that they are of the same stature as Europeans. The attainment of political independence is only one facet of their problem. The North African knows that when it comes to appreciating his culture, the average tourist cannot go much closer toward understanding it than a certain condescending curiosity. He realizes that, at best, to the European he is merely picturesque. Therefore, he reasons, to be taken seriously he must cease being picturesque. Traditional customs, clothing and behaviour must be replaced by something unequivocally European. In this he is fanatical. It does not occur to him that what he is rejecting is authentic and valid, and that what he is taking on is meaningless imitation. And if it did occur to him, it would not matter in the least. This total indifference to the cultural heritage everywhere appears to be a necessary adjunct to the early stages of nationalism.

Hospitality in North Africa knows no limits. You are taken in and treated as a member of the family. If you don't enjoy yourself, it is not your host's fault, but rather the result of your own inadaptability, for every attempt is made to see that you are happy and comfortable. Some time ago I was the guest of two brothers who had an enormous house in the Medina of Fez. So that I should feel truly at home, I was given an entire wing of the establishment, a tiled patio with a room on either side and a fountain in the centre. There were great numbers of servants to bring me food and drink, and also to inquire, before my hosts came to call, whether I was disposed to receive them. When they came they often brought singers and musicians to entertain me. The only hitch was that they went to such lengths to treat me as one of them that they also assumed I was not interested in going out into the city. During the entire fortnight I spent with them I never once found my way out of the house, or even out of my own section of it, since all doors were kept locked and bolted, and only the guard, an old Sudanese slave, had the keys. For long hours I sat in the patio listening to the sounds of the city outside, sometimes hearing faint strains of music that I would have given anything really to hear, watching the square of deep-blue sky above my head slowly become a softer and lighter blue as twilight approached, waiting for the swallows that wheeled above the patio when the day was finally over and the muezzins began their calls to evening prayer, and merely existing in the hope that someone would come, something would happen before too many hours had gone past. But as I say, if I was bored, that was my own fault and not theirs. They were doing everything they could to please me.

Just as in that Twelfth-Century fortress in Fez I had been provided with a small hand-wound phonograph and one record (Josephine Baker singing *J'ai Deux Amours*, a song hit of that year), so all over North Africa you are confronted with a mélange of the very old and the most recent, with no hint of anything left over from the intervening centuries. It is one of the great charms of the place, the fact that your today carries with it no memories of yesterday or the day before; everything that is not medieval is completely new. The younger generation of French and Jews, born and raised in the cities of North Africa, for the most part have no contact with that which is ancient in their countries. A Moroccan girl whose family moved from Rabat to New York, upon being asked what she thought of her new home, replied: "Well, of course, coming from a new country as I do, it's very hard to get used to all these old houses here in New York. I had no idea New York was so *old*". One is inclined to forget that the French began to settle in Morocco only at the time of World War I, and that the mushroom cities of Casablanca, Agadir and Tangier grew up in the 'thrities. Xauen, whose mountains are visible from the terrace of my apartment in Tangier, was entered by European troops for the first time in 1920. Even in southern Algeria, where one is inclined to think of the French as having been stationed for a much longer time, there are war monuments bearing battle dates as recent as 1912. Throughout the whole first quarter of the century the North African frontier was continuously being pushed southward by means of warfare, and south of the Grand Atlas it was 1936 before "pacification" came to an end and European civilians were allowed, albeit on the strict terms laid down by the military, to look for the first time into the magic valleys of the Draa, the Dadès and the Todra.

Appearing unexpectedly in out-of-the-way regions of North Africa has never been without its difficulties. I remember making an impossible journey before the last world war in a produce truck over the Grand Atlas to Ouarzazat, full of excitement at the prospect of seeing the Casbah there with its strange painted towers, only to be forced to remain three days inside the shack that passed for a hotel, and then sent on another truck straight back to Marrakech, having seen nothing but Foreign Legionnaires, and having heard no music other than the bugle calls that issued every so often from the nearby camp. Another time I entered Tunisia on camel back from across the Great Eastern Erg. I had two camels and one hard-working camel driver, whose job it was to run all day long from one beast to the other and try, by whacking their hind legs, to keep them walking in something resembling a straight line. This was a much more difficult task than it sounds; although our course was generally due east, one of the animals had an inexplicable desire to walk southward, while the other was possessed by an equally mysterious urge to go north. The poor man passed his time screaming; "Hut! Aïda!" and trying to run both ways at once. His turban was continually coming unwound, and he had no time to attend to the scarf he was knitting, in spite of the fact that he kept the yarn and needles dangling around his neck, ready to work on at any moment.

We did finally cross the border and amble into Tunisia, where we were immediately apprehended by the police. The camel driver and his beasts were sent back to Algeria where they belonged, and I started on my painful way up through Tunisia, where the French authorities evidently had made a concerted decision to make my stay in the country as wretched as possible. In the oasis at Nefta, in the hotel at Tozeur, even in the mosque of Sidi Oqba at Kairouan, I was arrested and taken off to the commissariat, carefully questioned, and told that I need not imagine I could make a move of which they would not be fully aware.

The explanation was that in spite of my American passport they were convinced I was a German; in those days anybody wandering around *l'Afrique Mineure*, (as one of the more erudite officers called this corner of the continent), if he did not satisfy the French idea of what a tourist should look like, was immediately suspect. Even the Moslems would look at me closely and say: "*Toi pas Fraçnais. Toi Allemand*," to which I never replied, for fear of having to pay the prices that would have been demanded if my true status had been revealed to them.

Algeria is a country where it is better to keep moving around than to stay long in one place. Its towns are not very interesting, but its landscapes are impressive. In the winter, travelling by train across the western steppes, you can go all day and see nothing but flat stretches of snow on all sides, unrelieved by trees in the foreground or by mountains in the distance. In the summer these same desolate lands are cruelly hot, and the wind swirls the dust into tall yellow pillars that move deliberately from one side of the empty horizon to the other. When you come upon a town in such regions, lying like the remains of a picnic lunch in the middle of an endless parking lot, you know it was the French who put it there. The Algerians prefer to live along the wild and beautiful sea-coast, in the palm gardens of the south, atop the cliffs bordering the dry rivers, or on the crests of the high mountains in the centre of the country. Up there above the slopes dotted with almond trees, the Berber villages sit astride the long spines of the lesser ranges. The men and women file down the zigzagging paths to cultivate the rich valleys below, here and there in full view of the snowfields where the French formerly had their skiing resorts. Far to the south lie the parallel chains of red sawtooth mountains which run northeast to southwest across the entire country and divide the plains from the desert.

No part of North Africa will again be the same sort of paradise for Europeans that it was during the first half of this century. The place has been thrown open to the Twentieth Century. With Europeanization and nationalism have come a consciousness of identity and the awareness of that identity's commercial possibilities. From now on the North Africans, like the Mexicans, will control and exploit their own charms, rather than being placed on exhibit for us by their managers, and the result will be a very different thing from what it has been in the past. Tourist land it is still, and doubtless will continue to be for a while, and it is on that basis only that we as residents or intending visitors are now obliged to consider it. We now come here as paying guests of the inhabitants themselves rather than of the exploiters. Travel here is certain not to be so easy or so comfortable as before, and prices are many times higher than they were, but at least we meet the people on terms of equality, which, we must admit, is a healthier situation.

If you live long enough in a place where the question of colonialism versus self-government is constantly being discussed, you are bound to find yourself having a very definite opinion on the subject. The difficulty is that some of your co-residents feel one way and some the other, but all feel strongly. Those in favour of colonialism argue that you can't "give" (quotes mine) an almost totally illiterate people political power and expect them to create a democracy, and that is doubtless true; but the point is that since they are inevitably going to take the power sooner or later, it is only reasonable to help them take it while they still have at least some measure of goodwill toward their erstwhile masters. The diehard French attitude is summed up in a remark made to me by a friendly immigration officer at the Algiers airport. "Our great mistake," he said sadly, "was ever to allow these savages to learn to read and write." I said I supposed that was a logical thing to say, if one expected to rule forever, which I knew, given the intelligence of the French, that they did not intend to try, since it was impossible. The official ceased looking sad and became much less friendly.

At a dinner in Marrakech during the French occupation, the Frenchman sitting beside me became engaged in an amicable discussion with a Moroccan across the table. "But look at the facts, *mon cher ami*. Before our arrival, there was constant warfare between the tribes. Since we came the population has doubled. Is that true or not?"

The Moroccan leaned forward. "We can take care of our own births and deaths," he said, smiling. "If we must be killed, just let other Moroccans attend to it. We really prefer that."

THE RIF, TO MUSIC •

The most important single element in Morocco's folk culture is its music. In a land like this, where almost total illiteracy has been the rule, the production of written literature is of course negligible. On the other hand, like the Negroes of West Africa the Moroccans have a magnificent and highly evolved sense of rhythm which manifests itself in the twin arts of music and the dance. Islam, however, does not look with favour upon any sort of dancing, and thus the art of the dance, while being the natural mode of religious expression of the native population, has not been encouraged here since the arrival of the Moslem conquerors. At the same time, the very illiteracy which through the centuries has precluded the possibility of literature has abetted the development of music: the entire history and mythology of the people is clothed in song. Instrumentalists and singers have come into being in lieu of chroniclers and poets, and even during the most recent chapter in the country's evolution – the war for independence and the setting up of the present pre-democratic regime – each phase of the struggle has been celebrated in countless songs.

The neolithic Berbers have always had their own music, and they still have it. It is a highly percussive art, with complicated juxtapositions of rhythms, limited scalar range (often of no more than three adjacent tones) and a unique manner of vocalizing. Like most Africans, the Berbers developed a music of mass-participation, one whose psychological effects were aimed more often than not at causing hypnosis. When the Arabs invaded the land they brought with them music of a very different sort, addressed to the individual, seeking by sensory means to induce a state of philosophical speculativeness. In the middle of Morocco's hostile landscape they built their great walled cities, where they entrenched themselves, and from which they sent out soldiers to continue the conquest, southward into the Sudan, northward into Europe. With the importation of large numbers of Negro slaves the urban culture

83

ceased being a purely Arabic one. (The child of a union between a female slave and her master was considered legitimate.) On the central plains and in the foothills of the mountains of the north the Berber music took on many elements of Arabic music, while in the pre-Sahara it borrowed from the Negroes, remaining a hybrid product in both cases. Only in the regions which remained generally inaccessible to non-Berbers – roughly speaking, the mountains themselves and the high plateaux, was Berber music left intact, a purely autochthonous art.

My stint, in attempting to record the music of Morocco, was to capture in the space of the six months which the Rockefeller Foundation allotted to me for the project, examples of every major musical genre to be found within the boundaries of the country. This required the close co-operation of the Moroccan government, everyone agreed. But with which branch of it? No one knew. Because the material was to belong to the archives of the Library of Congress in Washington, the American Embassy in Rabat agreed to help me in my efforts to locate an official who might be empowered to grant the necessary permission, for I needed a guarantee that I would be allowed to move freely about the untravelled parts of the country, and once in those parts, I needed the power to persuade the local authorities to find the musicians in each tribe and round them up for me.

We approached several ministries, some of which claimed to be in a position to grant such permission, but none of which was willing to give formal approval to the project. Probably there was no precedent for such an undertaking, and no one wanted to assume the responsibility of creating such a precedent. In desperation, working through personal channels, I managed eventually to evolve a document to which was stapled my photograph, with official stamps and signatures; this paper made it possible to start work. By this time it was early July. In October, when I had been at work for more than three months, I received a communication from the Ministry of Foreign Affairs which informed me that since my project was ill-timed I would not be allowed to undertake it. The American Embassy advised me to continue my work. By

December the Moroccan government had become aware of what was going on; they informed me summarily that no recordings could be made in Morocco save by special permission from the Ministry of the Interior. By then I had practically completed the project, and the snow was beginning to block the mountain passes, so this blow was not too bitter. However, from then on it was no longer possible to make any recordings which required the co-operation of the government; this deprived the collection of certain tribal musics of south-eastern Morocco. But I already had more than two hundred and fifty selections from the rest of the country, as diversified a body of music as one could find in any land west of India.

From Tangier, Christopher, Mohammed Larbi and I followed four roughly circular itineraries of five weeks' duration each: south-western Morocco, northern Morocco, The Atlas, and the pre-Sahara. Between trips we recuperated in Tangier. The pages which follow were written from day to day during the course of the second journey, most of whose days were spent in the mountains of the Rif.

—Alhucemas

August 29, 1959

The road to Ketama goes along the backbone of the western Rif. You can see for miles both to the Mediterranean side and to the southern side: big mountains and more big mountains. Mountains covered with olive trees, with oak trees, with bushes, and finally with giant cedars. For two or three hours before getting up to Ketama we had been passing large gangs of workmen repairing the road; repairs were badly needed. We had been going to cook lunch in a little pine grove just above a village between Bab Taza and Bab Berret, but when we got in among the trees, wherever we looked there were workmen lying on the dry pine needles in the shade, sleeping or smoking kif, so we set up our equipment in the sun and wind, a little below the crest where the pine grove was. The wind kept blowing out the butagaz flame, but in the end we managed to eat. Christopher drank his usual Chaudsoleil *rosé*, and Mohammed Larbi and I drank piping hot Pepsi-Cola, since there was no water left in the thermos we had filled in Xauen. That one thermosful proved to be the last good water we were to have for three weeks.

During lunch Mohammed Larbi insisted on amusing himself with the radio; he was trying to get Damascus on the nineteen-meter band in order to hear the news. When eventually he did get it he could not understand it, of course, because it was in Syrian Arabic, but that made no difference to him. It was news, and they were talking about Kassem and excoriating the French, which was easy enough for even me to understand. Mohammed Larbi had been smoking kif constantly all morning and was somewhat exalted. We packed up and started on our way again.

It was about half past four when we came in sight of the wide plain of Ketama they call Llano Amarillo. It is aptly named, at least in summer, for then it is dry and yellow. Here and there, scattered over a distance which went toward infinity, was a herd of cattle or a flock of sheep. They looked as though they had been put there purposely to give the place scale. At first you saw nothing but the yellow flatness with the great cedar trees along the sides. Then you saw the dots that were the nearest sheep, then to the right pinpoints that were cows, but smaller than the sheep, then far over to the left almost invisible specks that were another herd.

The *parador*, which has about twenty rooms, looked completely abandoned, but there was a chair on the wide front terrace, and the door was open. I went in to inquire about sleeping quarters. The inside seemed deserted too. The dining room had furniture in it; the other rooms had been stripped. In the town of Bab Berret, the Spanish, when they relinquished their protectorate, took the generator with them; the vicinity has been without electricity ever since. There was no sign of life at the reception desk, no piece of paper or ledger in sight, – nothing but keys hung in three rows on the wall. I called out: *"Hay alguien?"* and got no answer. Finally,

behind the big door of what had been the bar, I saw a pair of legs
lying on a decayed divan, and peered around the door. A young man
lay there with his eyes open, but he wasn't looking at me; he was
staring at the ceiling. When he did see me, he slowly sat up and
stretched a little, never answering my excuse me's and good afternoons. I decided he must be a guest and went out again into the
main hall, but in a minute he was there behind me, and then he
did not ask me what he could do for me, but what was the matter.

When he heard I wanted rooms he turned away with disgust on
his face. "There are no rooms," he said.

"None at all?"

"None at all."

"Is the hotel open?"

"The hotel's open and there are no rooms. Tomorrow you can
have some if you want."

"And tonight where am I going to sleep?"

He turned around again and looked at me blankly. Too much
kif; I could see that. He was scratching his crotch voluptuously
all this time. He yawned and began to walk toward the bar. "You
couldn't put up a cot somewhere?" I called after him. But he
continued to move away. I went out to the car to report. Christopher
and Mohammed Larbi came back in with me; they didn't believe
any of it.

The scratcher was already back on his broken-down couch,
getting himself into a comfortable position. This time he looked
really hostile. I decided to go back out onto the terrace. I didn't
want to see him any more. Mohammed Larbi was examining the
main entrance hall and the staircase. When Christopher came out
he said there were plenty of rooms, that the young man was finally
awake, and that we could stay after all. The foremen of the various
road construction gangs had requisitioned several rooms, (for
which they were not paying) but there were a dozen or more vacant
ones.

The scratcher was manager, bellboy, waiter, dishwasher and
accountant. Besides him there was a crazy-looking cook and an
old Riffian woman who made the beds and scrubbed the floors,

but that was the entire personnel. The cook also ran the generator in the garage; he took us out to admire it later on.

Someone had removed the doorknobs from the bedroom doors, so that if the door of your room happened to blow shut, you had to pound on it until the manager heard you and came upstairs with a piece of metal of his own fashioning which he stuck through the hole where the knob had been and turned the lock to let you either in or out, depending on where you happened to be. This was true of the hotel's one toilet, too, but that was of no importance because the place was so filthy that you didn't go into it anyway. The toilet bowl had been filled up and so people had begun using the floor. In 1950 I had spent a night in that one bathroom. They put a cot beside the tub and hung a scribbled sign on the door saying the bathroom was out of order, but that didn't prevent a steady stream of French tourists from pounding indignantly on the door throughout the long night. Some of them tried to break the door in, but the bolt was strong. Now that I stuck my head into the stinking room, I remembered that endless night and the noise of the unloading bus beneath my window at five in the morning, the bugle calls from the barracks back in the cedar forest and the gobbling of the turkeys out on the terrace.

We wanted to get down to Laazib Ketama as quickly as possible, in order to see the caid or the khalifa before the government offices closed, so we started out, bumping down the crazy, wide Tirak d'l Ouahada. Hundreds of Riffians, on horseback, muleback and donkeyback, the women walking, were on their way up. We covered them all with layers of white dust; there was no help for it. They were, however, in a fine humour, laughing and waving.

At one point you could look directly down from the road into a deep ravine whose sides were planted wholly with kif. Ketama is the kif centre of all North Africa, and very likely of the world now. It is the only region where it is legal to grow it, and that is because the Sultan has agreed to allow the cultivation of it to continue until the land has been made feasible for other crops. At present the only crop that will grow is kif, and it is Ketama which has been providing all the kif for Morocco – which means all the commercial kif. Anybody can plant a few stalks in his garden, but it's no good. The only really good kif is the Ketami. So you have miles and miles of it growing out of the stony soil on the edges of the steep slopes, and under the present ruling this will go on until some other means of livelihood has been found for the inhabitants.

At present the kif situation is ridiculous. Tons of the drug are grown each year and shipped out of Ketama in all directions. That is legal. But if anyone is caught selling it he is immediately given a heavy fine and/or a prison sentence. No penalties are attached to the possession of it, but the official attitude toward the smoking of it in public places differs according to the way the local authorities of each separate town feel about it. I was in Marrakech this month and found it wide open. In Fez I saw only one old man holding a sebsi. In Tangier and Tetuan clouds of kif smoke pour out of the cafes. In Rabat, Essaouira, Oujda, nothing. In some towns it's easy to get and cheap and good; in others, you might almost as well not even try. These conditions are of course far from static; they are constantly shifting. The city in which two months ago you could run around the corner for a paper of kif is suddenly closed tight, whereas in another town where previously there was strict vigilance, men are observed puffing on their pipes in the street, in full view of police headquarters. Generally speaking, when you get to the southern side of the Grand Atlas, kif is a luxury and greatly prized, whereas in the extreme north, among the Djebala, for instance, the average village male over fourteen has his little mottoui full of it and his sebsi in his pocket.

We stopped the car and climbed down a way to examine the phenomenon. None of us had ever before seen so much kif. We could have filled the back of the car with it and no one would have known. Mohammed Larbi stroked a stalk lovingly and murmured; "Like green diamonds everywhere. *Fijate*." An old man ambled by and sat down beside the road to look at us with curiosity. Mohammed Larbi shouted to him in Moghrebi: "Is this kif yours?" It was clear that next he was going to ask to be given some. But the old man did not understand. He merely stared at us. "Like donkeys!" snorted Mohammed Larbi. He never fails to be annoyed with the Riffians when they speak only Tarifcht; if a Moroccan does not understand at least some Moghrebi he takes it as a personal affront. When we got back to the car he pulled out his enormous sheep's bladder, packed with three pounds of the powerful greasy green kif he prepares himself, and filled a cigarette paper with it. "I've got to smoke!" he cried in great excitement. "I can't see all that kif and not feel some of it in me." He continued to smoke until we got down to Laazib Ketama.

The main body of the tribesmen had already left, (it was market day) but there were still several hundred men lying around on rugs and sacks under the cedars in the three big courtyards where the souk had been taking place. The merchants were winding bolts of cloth and packing sugar and toys and cutlery away into big bundles. The dust that hung in the air, where it came in contact with the last rays of the sun, made blinding golden streamers across the scene. We sneezed repeatedly as we picked our way through the emptying market. There were the customary blank faces when we inquired after the khalifa's office, but we found it, and eventually managed to get into it. I had forgotten about the short war of 1958 between the Riffians and the forces of the Rabat government, but the memory of it came back soon enough. They told me that since we were in a military zone we would have to consult the comandante if we expected to be allowed to record. Yes, the comandante had been down here in Laazib Ketama all day, but now he had left, and who knew where he was now? However, they were building a bridge just below the village, and perhaps he was down there watching. We went further down the trail. It looked a hopeless task to find anyone in the midst of such chaos. In any case, it was already twilight and we had about fifteen miles of rough trail to climb in order to get back to the *parador*. So we backed up, nearly went over a small cliff, and headed upward toward Llano Amarillo.

Because the khalifa had also suggested that we stop off at the barracks on the way back to the *parador* in the event that the comandante might be there, we turned in toward a three-storey log cabin that looked like an expensive hotel in a ski-ing resort, and were met by a dozen wide-eyed Moroccan youths in uniform who immediately trained their submachine guns on us, just in case it turned out that we needed to be captured. A sergeant made them back up, and told us that the comandante would be coming in about eight o'clock.

The khalifa in Laazib Ketama had mentioned a village some thirty kilometers further on where there were some rhaita players. His news did not stimulate me particularly, because I already had taped a good many sequences of rhaita music, including some excellent ones from Beni Aros, the musical capital of Djebala musicians. The rhaita among the Djebala is not noticeably different from the rhaita in the Rif, save perhaps that the Riffians' playing shows a more accurate rhythmical sense. What I was looking for was the *zamar*, a double reed instrument fitted with a pair of bull's horns. The khalifa had assured me that the Beni Uriaghel in the Central Rif would supply that; for lack of anything better I had shown polite interest in his offer of *rhaitas*, and I was ready to devote a day to recording them. It would depend upon whether the comandante proved willing to collect the musicians for me; I did not want to waste any energy or time having to persuade him, even if it meant no recording in the Ketama region. I was eager to get on eastward to where the true Riffian music is.

We drove back to the hotel. The mountain night had settled over the valley. The wind was whistling through the rooms; doors were squeaking and banging all by themselves. Each minute I was becoming less interested in finding the comandante. We went to my room and turned on the shivering little electric light bulb over the bed. Christopher and Mohammed Larbi make a habit of meeting in my room because I have the equipment with me: the two tape recorders, the radio, the food and drink, and the fire. There is seldom a reason for either of them ever to go to his own room save to sleep. On our twilight visit to the generator in the garage we had learned that it supplied two hundred twenty volt direct current to the *parador*, and so I already knew that it was not going to be possible to work the tape recorders, either for studying tapes already recorded or for our amusement. This was bad news. The night would be cold and uncomfortable, once we were in those forbidding beds. We needed a reason to stay up late.

Ketama is fairly high for the Rif: about six thousand feet up. With the setting of the sun a mountain chill had crept down through the forest from the heights. The road menders were eating sardines in their rooms. It was cold in the empty *comedor* at dinner time. As soon as we had eaten we went upstairs and made coffee. Mohammed Larbi brought out the bottle of Budapest kümmel, and Christopher handed us the half-kilo bag of *majoun* someone had sold him in Xauen. We all drank kümmel, but only Mohammed Larbi ate any majoun. If someone is entirely comfortable and contented, majoun can enhance his pleasure, but there is no point in italicizing an unsatisfactory experience.

It suddenly occurred to me that the lights might be turned off, and that we had no candles. I went down to look for the manager. He was drying dishes in the kitchen with the cook, who was smoking kif in a very long sebsi. I was right, he said; the lights would be going off within twenty minutes, at ten o'clock, and there were no candles in the *parador*. That I did not believe. I objected that there must be at least one, somewhere.

"No candles," he said, firmly.

"Haven't you got a piece of one?"

"No pieces of candles," he replied, drying dishes, not looking up. "Nothing."

It was clearly a provocation. I had seen what had happened when I had tried to get the rooms. Christopher had been able to get them out of him; I had not, and he was aware of this. He was playing his inexplicable little game again. I stood there. Finally I said: "I don't understand this hotel."

Now he set down his dish and turned to face me. "*Señor*," he said deliberately, "don't you know this is the worst hotel in the world?"

"What?"

He repeated the words slowly: "It's the worst hotel in the world."

"No, I didn't know," I said. "Who owns it?"

"A poor slob who lives around here." He and the cook exchanged mysterious, amused glances. I could think of nothing to retort save that I had been under the impression that it was run by the government. Formerly it was the family or religion that one criticised, if in the course of one's personal relations one found it expedient to infuriate a Moroccan; nowadays one gets the same reaction by ridiculing the government, since at last it is Moroccans who are responsible for it. But neither one of them understood my remark as the insult I had intended. "No, no, no!" they laughed. "Just a *pobre desgraciado.*"

I went back upstairs and reported all this; it was greeted with loud laughter. Christopher got up and left the room. A minute or two later he was back with three new candles and two half-burned ones. The lights stayed on until half-past ten. We went to bed. In the morning there was a blinding fog and it was still cold. I had a hacking cough, and decided that I must be about to come down with something. Christopher and Mohammed Larbi came in and made coffee. I told them I wanted no music from Ketama; we were leaving immediately for Alhucemas. When I went down to pay the bill, for the first time the manager looked nearly awake. I got back my change, and out of curiosity I handed him two hundred francs as a tip, determined, if he threw the coins on the floor, merely to pick them up and leave. But his face suddenly came alive.

"I'm going crazy here," he confided. "How can I do anything? There's nothing here, nothing works, everything's broken, there's no money, nobody comes but road workers. Anybody would go crazy."

I nodded in sympathy.

"I'll be leaving soon, of course," he continued. "I'm not used to places like this. I'm from Tetuan."

"Is that so?"

"I've been here two months almost, but next week I'm getting out."

"I'd say that's lucky for you." I did not believe he would really be leaving, although at the moment he looked passionate enough to walk out of the door and down the highway, and never return.

Some Moroccans can work themselves into a state of emotional unbalance with astonishing speed.

"I'm going, all right. You've got to be crazy to live up here. *Ma'al akhorine.*"

I said good-bye and he wished me good luck.

The road east of Ketama was extremely bad: a rough surface sprinkled with small sharp stones. An unbanked curve every few yards. At times the fog was so thick that nothing at all was visible but the dirt bed of the road (and the stones everywhere on it) three feet ahead of the car. We crawled along. The fog dissolved. There were villages down in the valleys at our feet. The earth was whitish grey, and so were the enormous square earthen houses. Traditional Riffian architecture, untouched. The landscape was timeless.

We bought gasoline in Targuist. The place was the last refuge of poor old Abd el Krim; the French captured him here in 1926. Many Jews, speaking Spanish. The modern town a monstrous excrescence with long dirty streets; the wind blowing along them, whipping clouds of dust and filth against the face, stinging the skin. The Moslem village across the highway of a more attractive aspect, but unreachable in the car. Beyond Targuist a dark sky and a high wind and a country-side which grew more arid and forlorn by the mile. Finally it was raining, but the storm passed in time for us to make our lunch beside a culvert where the dirt in the wind cut less (for in this valley it had not rained), and where we could keep the flame of the butagaz alive.

We drove into Alhucemas here about half past four. The sea looked like lead. The town itself has a certain paranoid quality: the classic Spanish fishing village seen as in a bad dream. A vague atmosphere of impending disaster, of being cut off from the world, as in a penal colony. A penal colony, yes. It is in the faces of the few Spaniards sitting in the shabby cafés. Most of the *Spanioline* have gone away. The ones who remain are not likely to admit that the only reason they are still here is that it is impossible for them to go anywhere else.

The Moroccans have taken over Alhucemas – all of it except

94

the Hotel España. I am in a luxurious room with a tile shower; there is hot water in the pipes. It is unbelievable, the first since Tangier. The weather remains lowering, and suddenly it is dark. At dinner the fat Spanish waiter is the principal source of amusement: he is definitely drunk, and even staggers classically as he brings in the food. Mohammed Larbi makes fairly brutal fun of him all through the meal.

The next morning we go to see the Governor. He is friendly, speaks in Tarifcht to his assistants; in the government offices of the south they are likely to use French. He says that tomorrow evening we are to report to the fort at Ajdir. There the Caid of Einzoren will meet us and take over. We have agreed. The sky is still dark and the air heavy.

—Alhucemas

August 31, 4 a.m.

The *Caid* of Einzoren proved to be a jolly young man from Rabat, not much more than twenty years old. He is enjoying himself enormously up here in the Rif, he confided, because he has a girl in Einzoren, a "hundred per-cent Española" named Josefina. In the middle of our recording session he invited us to have dinner with him and Josefina. We accepted, but were given a table where we sat alone eating the food he had ordered for us, while he sat with Josefina and her family.

We had set up the recording equipment in an empty municipal building which stood in the middle of the main plaza. It gave the impression of being a school which was no longer in use. When we arrived, we found one of the rooms already filled with women and girls, three dozen or so of them, singing and tapping lightly on their drums. They sat in straight-backed chairs, their heads and shoulders entirely hidden under the bath towels they wore. A great hushed crowd of men and boys stood outside in the plaza, pressing against the building, trying to peer over the high windowsills. Now and then someone whispered; I was grateful for their silence.

The tribe was the Beni Uriaghel, but in spite of that there was no zamar. It was a great disappointment. I questioned the *caid* about the possibilities of finding one. He knew even less than I about it; he had never suspected the existence of such an instrument. The musicians themselves shook their heads: the Beni Uriaghel did not use it, they said. Not even in the country, I pursued, outside Einzoren? They laughed, because they were all rustics from the mountains roundabout, and had been summoned to the village to take part in the "festival."

No one had told me that the girls were going to sing in competitive teams, or that each village would be represented by two rival sets of duo-vocalists, so that I was not prepared for the strange aspect of the room. They sat in pairs, their heads close enough together so that each couple could be wholly covered by the one large turkish towel. The voices were directed floorward through the folds of cloth, and since no gesture, no movement of the head, accompanied the singing, it was literally impossible to know who was performing and who was merely sitting. The song was surprisingly repetitious even for Berber music; nevertheless I was annoyed to have it marred by the constant sound of murmurs and whispers and *sotto voce* remarks during the performance, an interference the microphone would inevitably register. But there was no way of catching anyone's eye, since no eyes were visible. Even the matrons, who where supplying the drumming, were covered. The first selection went on and on, strophe after strophe, the older women tapping the membranes of their disc-shaped *benadir* almost inaudibly on arbitrary offbeats. I took advantage of the piece's length to leave the controls and go over to whisper a question to the *caid*, who sat beaming in an honorific armchair, flanked by his subordinates, crouching on the floor around him. "Why are they all talking so much?" I asked him.

He smiled. "They're making up the words they're going to sing next," he told me. I was pleased to hear that the texts were improvised, and went back to my Ampex and earphones to wait for the song to end. When the girls had gone on for thirty-five minutes more, and the tape had run out, I tiptoed across the room once again to the *caid*. "Are all the pieces going to be this long?" I inquired.

"Oh they'll go on until I stop them," he said. "All night, if you like."

"The same song?"

"Oh, yes. It's about me. Do you want them to sing a different one?"

I explained that it was no longer being recorded, and he called a halt. After that I was able to control the length of the selections.

Presently word arrived that the rhaita group was sitting in a café somewhere at the edge of town, waiting for transportation, and so, accompanied by a cicerone, Christopher drove out to fetch them. The café proved to be in a village about twenty kilometers distant. The men were playing when he arrived; when he told them to get into the car they did so without ceasing to play. They played all the way to Einzoren, and walked into the building where I was without having interrupted the piece. I let them finish it, and then had them taken back outside into the public square. Mohammed Larbi carried the microphone out and set it up in the middle of the great circle formed by the male onlookers. The *rhaita*, a super-oboe whose jagged, strident sound has been developed precisely for long-distance listening, is not an indoor instrument.

While we were away in the restaurant, the men and the women in the public square somehow got together and put on a *fraja*. This would not have happened in the regions of Morocco where Arab culture has been imposed on the population, but in the Rif it is not considered improper for the two sexes to take part in the same entertainment. Even here the men did not dance; they played, sang and shouted while the women danced. I heard the racket from the restaurant and hurried back to try and tape it, but as soon as they saw what I was doing they became quiet. There was a group of excellent musicians from a village called Tazourakht; their music was both more primitive and more precise rhythmically than that of the others, and I showed open favouritism in asking for more of it. This proved to be not too good an idea, for they were the only men to belong to another tribe, the Beni Bouayache.

97

The recording session, which had been in progress since dusk, gave signs of being about to degenerate into a wild party somewhere around two o'clock in the morning. I suggested to the *caid* that we stop, but he saw no reason for that. At twenty to three we disconnected the machines and packed them up. "We're going on with this until tomorrow," said the *caid*, declining our offer of a ride to Alhucemas. The sounds of revelry were definitely growing louder as we drove away.

—Alhucemas
August 31

Last night was really enough; we ought to go on eastward. But the Governor has gone out of his way to be helpful, and has arranged another session in Ismoren, a village in the hills to the west, for tomorrow evening. Today I succeeded in enticing the two Riffian maids at the hotel here into my room to help me identify sixteen pieces on a tape I recorded in 1956. I knew it was all music from the Rif, but I wanted to find out which pieces were from which tribes, in order to have a clearer idea of what each genre was worth in terms of the effort required to capture it. The girls refused to come into the room without a chaperone; they found a thirteen year-old boy and brought him with them. This was fortunate, because the boy spoke some Moghrebi, while they knew only Tarifcht and a few words of Spanish. I would play a piece and they would listen for a moment before identifying its source. Only two pieces caused them any hesitation, and they quickly agreed on those. I still need examples of the Beni Bouifrour, the Beni Touzine, the Ait Ulixxek, the Gzennaia and the Temsaman. The girls were delighted with the small sum I gave them; upon leaving the room they insisted on taking some soiled laundry with them to wash for me.

—Nador
September 6

We went up to Ismoren as scheduled, at twilight on the following day. The landscape reminded me of central Mexico. The trail from the highway up to the village was a constant slow climb along a wide tilting plain. The *caid* was not at home; there had been a misunderstanding and he was in Alhucemas. The villagers invited us into his home, saying the musicians were ready to play when we wanted to begin. It was a Spanish house with large rooms, dimly lit and sparsely furnished. There were great piles of almonds lying about in the corners; they reached almost up to the ceiling. The dank odour they gave off made the place smell like an abandoned farmhouse. The feeble electricity trembled and wavered. I had Mohammed Larbi test the current because I suspected it of being direct. Unhappily, that was what it proved to be, and I had to announce that in spite of all the preparations it was not going to be possible to record in Ismoren. There was incredulity and then disappointment on all faces. "Stay the night," they told us, "and tomorrow perhaps the electric force will be better." I thanked them and said we could not do that, but Mohammed Larbi, exasperated by their ignorance, launched into an expository monologue on electricity. Nobody listened. Men were beginning to bang drums outside on the terrace, and someone who looked like the local schoolteacher was delegated to serve tea. He invited me to preside at the *caid's* big desk. When they saw me sitting there, they laughed. An elderly man remarked: "He makes a good caid," and they all agreed. I opened three packs of cigarettes and passed them around. Everyone was looking longingly at the equipment, wanting very much to see it set up. We had tea, more tea, and still more tea, and finally got off for Alhucemas to a noisy accompaniment of *benadir*, with two men running ahead to us along the cactus-bordered lanes to show us the way out of the village.

And so each morning I continued to go down to the government offices to study their detailed wall maps and try to locate the tribes with which I hoped to make contact. (The first day I had spotted an official surreptitiously looking up our police records; apparently they were satisfactory.) The Governor and his aides had begun with a maximum of cordiality. But as the novelty of seeing us wore off, their attitude underwent a metamorphosis. It seemed to them that we were being arbitrary and difficult in our insistence upon certain tribes instead of others, and they had had enough of telephoning and making abortive arrangements. (It involved about two hours' work for them each day.) It was the electricity which frustrated us every time; we had been supplied with a transformer but not with a generator, and Einzoren appeared to be the only village in the region with alternating current.

One night when we went in to have dinner in the *comedor* of the Hotel España there was a murderous-looking soldier sitting at the table with Mohammed Larbi. We sat down; he was drunk and wanted to deliver a political lecture. He and Mohammed Larbi went out together. At three in the morning there was a great racket in the corridors. Mohammed Larbi was finding the way to his room with the help of various recruits from the street and with the voluble hindrance of the hotel's night watchman. The next day, which had been set as the day of departure, he was moaning sick. He managed to pack the car for us, and then fell into the back with the luggage, to say no more. The weather had gone on being dramatic and threatening. South of Temsaman the mountains, even in normal weather, look like imaginary sketches of another planet. Under the black sky and with the outrageous lighting effects that poured through unexpected valleys, they were a disquieting sight. Mohammed Larbi moaned occasionally.

The trail was execrable, but fortunately we did not meet another car all day – at least, not until late afternoon when we had got down into the plain to Laazib Midar, where a real road is suddenly born. My idea was to find some sort of place thereabouts where we could stay when we returned after seeing the Governor at Nador (since we were now in the Province of Nador and had to go all the way to the capital to get permission to work). But, Laazib Midar being only a frontier – like agglomeration of small adobe houses strung along the road, we went on through.

From the back seat Mohammed Larbi began once more to wail. "*Ay, yimma habiba*! Ay, what bad luck!" I told him that nobody had forced him to drink whatever he had drunk. "But they did!" he lamented. "That's just what happened. I was forced." I laughed unsympathetically. No one can smoke as much kif as Mohammed

Larbi does and be able to drink, too. I thought it was time he knew it, inasmuch as he has been smoking regularly since he was eleven, and he is now twenty-five.

"But it was at the barracks, and there were eight soldiers, and they said if I didn't drink I must be a woman. Is that *b'd drah* or not?"

"It's very sad," I said, and he was quiet.

It was black night and raining quietly when we got into Nador. After driving up and down the muddy streets we stopped at a grocery store to ask about a hotel. A Spaniard in the doorway said there was no hotel, and that we should go on to Melilla. That was completely out of the question, since Melilla, although in Morocco, has been Spanish for the past four hundred and fifty years, and still is; even if Christopher and Mohammed Larbi had been in possession of Spanish visas, which they were not, we could never have got the equipment across the border. I said we had to stay in Nador no matter what. The Spaniard said: "Try Paco Gonzalez at the gasoline pump. He might put you up. He's a European, at least."

A small Moroccan boy who was listening shouted: "Hotel Mokhtar is good!" The word *hotel* interested me, and we set out in search of it. Less than an hour later we came across it; it was over a Moslem café. Above the door someone had printed in crooked letters: H. MOKHTAR. The place reminds me somewhat of the Turkish baths that used to exist in the Casbah of Algiers thirty years ago. It is run by a bevy of inquisitive Riffian women; I know there are a great many of them, but I haven't yet been able to distinguish one from the others. They all came, one at a time, to examine our luggage and equipment; then apparently they held a conference, after which they put a "kitchen" at our disposal. This room was strewn with garbage, but it had two grids where charcoal fires could be built if you had charcoal. It also had a sink which was stopped up and full, I should guess, of last year's dishwater. We threw the garbage out the window onto the flowers in the patio, (there was nowhere else to put it) and installed ourselves. By now we are used to inhaling the stench of the latrines at each breath, but that first night it bothered us considerably. I flung my window open and discovered that the air outside was worse. The interior odour was of ancient urine, but the breeze that entered through the window brought a heavy scent of fresh human excrement. Just how that could be was unascertainable for the moment. However, I shut the window and lighted several *bathi* sticks, and then we settled down to prepare some food.

The next morning when I looked out into the sunlight I understood. The Hotel Mokhtar is built at the edge of town; for about five hundred yards beyond it the earth is crisscrossed by trenches three feet deep. These are the town's lavatories; at any moment during the day you can always see a dozen or more men, women and children squatting in the trenches. Until 1955 Nador was just another poor Moroccan village with a few Spaniards in it; suddenly it was made the capital of a newly designated province. The Spanish still have several thousand troops stationed here to "protect" Melilla, (which Rabat more or less openly claims and will undoubtedly sooner or later recover). And so, naturally enough, the Moroccans have that many thousand soliders plus several thousand more, quartered here in order to protect Nador. There are many more people here than there should be. Water has to be got in pails and oil-tins from pumps in the street; food is at a premium and all commodities are scarce. Dust hangs over the town and refuse surrounds it, except on the east, where the shallow waters of the Mar Chica lap against the mud, disturbing the dead fish that unaccountably float there in large numbers. The Mar Chica is a useless inland sea with an average depth of about six feet – just enough to drown a man. At the horizon, glistening and white, is the sandbar where the Mediterranean begins, and toward which one gazes wistfully, imagining the clean-smelling breeze that must sometimes blow out there. Nador is a prison. The presence of a wide, palm-and-flower-planted boulevard leading down the half-mile from the adminstration building to the dead shore of the Mar Chica only makes the place more revolting. At the lower end of the thoroughfare is a monstrous edifice built to look like a huge juke-box, and supported by piles that raise it above the water. This is the town's principal restaurant, where we eat each noon. The *paseo* is lined with roadside cafés and concrete benches. When the benches are full of the hundreds of desperate-looking Spanish and Moroccan soldiers who roam the streets, the only place for new arrivals to sit is in the chairs put out under the palms by the café-keepers. They sit there, but they stare down the boulevard and order nothing. At night it's a little less depressing because the thoroughfare is not at all well lighted and the intense shabbiness does not show. Besides, after dark the two military populations are shut into their respective barracks.

The first day here we went to the Governor's office; he was in Meknès with the Sultan, but his voluble *katib* had stayed behind, and it was he who took charge of us. "Let's see. You want the Beni Bouifrour tribe. You will have them tomorrow without fail. Go now to Segangan."

That sounded too easy. He saw my hesitation. "You can still catch the *khalifa* before he goes out for his *aperitif*. Wait. I shall telephone him. He will wait." And when I looked dubious, "By my order he will wait. Go."

("To get us out of the way," I thought. "When we come back, this one will be gone, and I'll lose the whole day. Maybe two days.") My doubt must have made itself even more noticeable, for he became dramatic. "I am telephoning. Now. Look. My hand is on the telephone. As soon as you go out of that door I shall speak with the *khalifa*. You can go with the certainty that I shall keep my word." I understood that the longer I listened to him go on in this vein, the less I was going to believe anything that he said. There seemed to be nothing to do but start out for Segangan immediately.

But the *katib* had telephoned, after all, and the *khalifa* of Segangan, once we found the military headquarters where he had his office, proved to be pleasant and unreserved. He closed his office and walked with us into the street. As we strolled under the acacias he said: "We have many charming gardens here in Segangan." (He pronounced it Azrheung-ng'n, in the Riffian fashion.) "It only remains for you to choose the garden of your preference for the recording."

"Haven't you a room somewhere?" I suggested. "It would be quieter, and besides, I need to plug my equipment into the electric current."

"Gardens are better than rooms," he said. "And we have our own electrician who will do whatever you ask him."

We examined bowers and arbours and fountains and nooks. I explained that I did not care where we did it, if outside noises were kept at a minimum, and that bearing this in mind, it seemed that indoors would perhaps be preferable.

"Not at all!" cried the *khalifa*. "I shall have all traffic deflected during the recording."

"But then the people of the town will know something is going on, and they'll come to find out what it is, and there will be more noise than ever!"

"No, no," he said reassuringly. "Foot traffic will not be allowed to circulate."

It was clear that any such measures would call attention to us straightaway, because they never would be fully enforced. But his excessive proposals were a part of his desire to appear friendly, and so I ceased objecting, and resolved to speak to the *katib* about it when I got back here to Nador. We found a place in which to record, a remote corner of one of the parks, as shady as a thicket, and quiet save for the crowing of roosters in the distance. The session was arranged for tomorrow morning. Back here in Nador I went to find the katib, but he had left his office for the day; we shall be at the mercy of the well-meaning *khalifa*.

—Nador

September 7

My anxiety was unnecessary. When we got to Nador this morning, we were taken to a completely different garden, quite outside the town. The *khalifa's* electrician had already installed the cable, and everything went with beautiful smoothness.

Among the Berbers, not only in the Rif, but much further south in the Grand Atlas, the professional troubador still exists; the social category allotted him is not exactly that of an accepted member of the community, but neither is he a pariah. As an entertainer he is respected; as an itinerant worker he is naturally open to some suspicion. The Riffians are fond of drawing an analogy between the *imdyazen* (as the minstrels are called both here and in the Atlas) and the *gitanos* of Spain – only, as they point out, the *imdyazen* live in houses like other people, and not in camps outside the towns like the gypsies. If you ask them why that is, they will usually reply: "Because they are of the same blood as we." In Segangan I had my first encounter with the *imdyazen*. Their chikh looked like a well-chosen extra in a pirate film – an enormous, rough, good-natured man with a bandanna around his head instead of a turban. He, at last, had a *zamar* with him. Even Mohammed Larbi had never seen one before. We examined it at some length, and photographed it from various angles. It consists of two separate reed pipes wired together, each with its own mouthpiece and perforations; fitted to the end of each reed is a large bull's horn. The instrument can be played with or without the horns, which are easily detached. Yesterday the effusive *khalifa* promised me two *zamars*, and even this morning he let me go on believing, for the first half hour or so, that a second player would be forthcoming. But when I began to seem anxious about his arrival and made inquiries among some of the officials, meaningful glances were exchanged, and the language abruptly shifted from Moghrebi into Tarifcht. I realized then that I was being boorish; one does not bring a lie out into the open. For some personal reason the *chikh* did not want another *zamar*, and that was that. He was an expert on his instrument, and he played it in every conceivable manner: standing, seated, while dancing, with horns, without, in company with drums and vocal chorus, and as a solo. He insisted on playing it even when I asked him not to. Within two hours my principal problem was to make him stop playing it, because its sound covered that of the other instruments to such an extent that there was a danger of monotony in sonorous effect. I finally seated him ten or twelve yards away from the other musicians. He went on playing, his cheeks puffed out like balloons, sitting all alone under an orange tree, happily unaware that his music was not being recorded.

One very good reason why I wanted to cut out the *zamar* was the presence among the players of an admirable musician named Boujemaa ben Mimoun, one of the few North African instrumentalists I have seen who had an understanding of the concept of personal expression in interpretation. His instrument was the *qsbah*, the long reed flute with the low register, common in the Sahara of southern Algeria but not generally used in most parts of Morocco. I had been trying to get a *qsbah* solo ever since I had found a group of Rhmara musicians in Tetuan. The Rhmara had agreed to do it, but their technique was indifferent and their sound was not at all what I had hoped for. Again I tried at Einzoren, and got good results musically, but once more not in the deep octave, which because of the demands it makes on breath control is the most difficult register to manage.

When I drew Boujemaa ben Mimoun aside and asked him if he would be willing to play a solo, he was perplexed. He wanted to please me, but as he said: "How is anybody going to know what the *qsbah* is saying all by itself, unless there is somebody to sing the words?" The *chikh* saw us conferring together, and came over to investigate. When he heard my request, he immediately proclaimed that the thing was impossible. Ben Mimoun hastily agreed with him. I continued to record, but clandestinely carried my problem to the *caid* of the village from which the imdyazen had been recuited. He was sitting, smoking kif with some other notables in a small pergola nearby. He seemed to think that a *qsbah* could play alone if it were really necessary. I assured him that it was, that the American government wished it. After a certain length of time spent in discussion, during which Mohammed Larbi passed out large quantities of kif to everyone, the experiment was made. The *chikh* saved face by insisting that two versions of each number be made – one for *qsbah* solo and one with sung text. I was delighted with the results. The solos are among the very best things in the collection. One called *Reh dial Beni Bouhiya* is particularly beautiful. In a landscape of immensity and desolation it is a moving thing to come upon a lone camel-driver sitting beside his fire at night while the camels sleep, and listen for a long time to the querulous, hesitant cadences of the *qsbah*. The music, more than any other I know, most completely expresses the essence of solitude. *Reh dial Beni Bouhiya* is a perfect example of the genre. Ben Mimoun looked unhappy while he played, because there was a tension in the air caused by general disapproval of my procedure. Everyone sat quietly, however, until he had finished.

After that they went back to ensemble playing and dancing. The kif had sharpened not only their sense of rhythm but their appetites as well, and I could see that we had come to the end of the session. As the drummers frantically leapt about, nearly tripping over the microphone cable, a tall man in a fat turban approached the microphone and began to shout directly into it. "It's a dedication," explained the *caid*. First there was praise of the Sultan, Mohammed Khamiss, as well as of his two sons, Prince Moulay Hassan and Prince Moulay Abdallah. After that came our friend the Governor of Alhucemas Province, (because in the 1958 Riffian war of dissidence he found a solution which pleased nearly everybody) and finally, with the highest enthusiasm, came a glorification of the Algerian fighters who are being slaughtered by the French next door, may Allah help them. (drums and shouting, and the bulls' horns pointing toward the sky, spouting wild sound). We drank far too much tea, and got back here to Nador too late to eat in the juke-box restaurant on stilts, so we opened some baked beans and ate them in the filth and squalor of my room.

—Nador
September 10

Mohammed Larbi is still fairly ill as a result of his experience in Alhucemas; his liver is not functioning properly, and he is trying to remedy it by doubling the amount of kif he smokes. The device is not working. It does however have one advantage: the stink of urine in the corridor is somewhat tempered by the overpowering but cleaner smell of burning kif, particularly if he leaves his door open, a habit I am trying to encourage. He lies in his room all day on the bed in an intense stupor, somewhere above the stratosphere, with the radio tuned constantly into either Cairo or Damascus. We cook breakfast and supper in my room, which gradually has come to look like a stall in any Moroccan joteya, with the most diverse objects covering every square foot of floor space. The only way I can get out of bed is to climb over the footboard and land in front of the lavabo. Each day several of the bright-eyed Riffian proprietresses come and look in happily, saying: "We don't have to make up the room today, either?" The bed has never yet been made, and the floor never swept; I don't want anyone in the room.

This morning Mohammed Larbi's sickness put him in mind of the time his stepmother tried to poison him. This is a favourite story of his which he recounts often and graphically. It seems to have been a traumatic experience for him, and this is scarcely surprising. As a result of it he walked out the door of his home and remained in hiding from his family for more than five years. It is merely incidental that during that time he married two former prostitutes: they were the only girls he knew personally. All others were potential poisoners. To him they still are; his fulminations against human females are hair-raising.

It appears that his mother left his father when the latter took a fourth wife, because although she had put up with the other two, she did not want to live in the house with the latest addition. So she packed up and went back to Tcharhanem where she had a little mud hut with nothing in it but a straw pallet and some earthenware pots. Mohammed Larbi stayed on with his father and the other wives. The new one, being the youngest, tried to get him into bed with her while Father was away from the house, and being a normally moral young man he indignantly refused. The girl was then overcome by fear that he might talk, and so she decided to get rid of him. Soon one day she pretended that something had gone wrong with the lunch, and that she would have to cook it again. It was half past four in the afternoon before she appeared with Mohammed Larbi's food. She was counting, and correctly, on his being more than ordinarily hungry. However, while he was wolfing his meal he caught sight of a bit of thread sticking out of the meat in the middle of the *tajine*. He pulled on it to no avail, and finally bit into the meat. It was only then that it occured to him what the string might mean, and he ripped open the meat with his fingers, to find that a small inner pocket of meat enclosing various powders and other things had been sewn into the larger piece. He also discovered that he had eaten a certain amount of that pocket and its contents. He said nothing, scrambled up off the floor, and ran out of the house, and to this day he has never been back there, although subsequently he did manage to persuade his father to get rid of that particular wife. The "other things" in the food, in addition to the assorted drugs, were, by his reluctant admission, powdered fingernails and finely cut hair – pubic hair, he maintains – along with bits of excrement from various small creatures. "Like what?" I wanted to know. "Like bats, mice, lizards, owls . . . How should I know what women find to feed to men?" he cried aggrievedly. At the end of a month his skin began to slough off, and one arm turned bluish purple. That is usual; I have seen it on occasion. It is also considered a good sign: it means that the poison is "coming out". The concensus of opinion is that if it stays in, there is not much that anyone can do in the way of finding an antidote.

The poisons are provided by professionals; Larache is said to be a good place to go if you are interested in working magic on somebody. You are certain to come back with something efficacious. Every Moroccan male has a horror of *tseuheur*. Many of them, like Mohammed Larbi, will not eat any food to which a Moslem woman has had access beforehand, unless it be his mother or sister, or, if he really trusts her, his wife. But too often it is the wife of whom he must be the most careful. She uses *tseuheur* to make him malleable and suggestible. It may take many months, or even several years, but the drugs are reliable. Often it is the central nervous system which is attacked. Blindness, paralysis, imbecility or dementia may occur, although by that time the wife probably has gone off to another part of the country. If the husband dies, there is no investigation. His hour has come, nothing more. Even though the practice of magic is a punishable offence, in the unlikely event that it can be proven, hundreds of thousands of men live in daily dread of it. Fortunately Mohammed Larbi is sure of his present wife; he beats her up regularly and she is terrified of him. "She'll never try to give me *tseuheur*," he boasts. "I'd kill her beofre she had it half made." This story is always essentially the same, but at each telling I gather a few more descriptive details.

"That's why I can't drink any more," he laments. "It's the *tseuheur* still in there somewhere, and it turns the drink to poison."

"It's the kif," I tell him.

—Nador
September 13

The cough that began at Ketama is still with me. The dry air at Alhucemas helped to keep it somewhat in abeyance; the conditions here in the Hotel Mokhtar seem to aggravate it. However, it is too late to leave for the present, because I feel feverish.

—Nador
September 15

Two days later. Still in bed, but much better. Christopher is disgusted with the situation, and Mohammed Larbi is in a state of advanced disintegration. The idea of going back to Midar does not bother me so much as knowing that after that we shall have to return here to Nador once again. The pail of dark water provided for us by the women, out of which I have been filling empty wine bottles with Halazone tablets in them, so we could have some kind of water to drink, proved to have a large, indescribably filthy cleaning rag buried in the silt at the bottom. I discovered it only this morning when all the water had been drunk. At that moment I wanted more than anything merely to escape from here. During lunch I said tentatively: "What do you think of going east, soon?" Christopher thought well of the idea, and so did Mohammed Larbi. I have renounced Temsaman, the Beni Touzine and the Ait Ulixxek.

Even the weather seemed brighter when we had left Nador behind and were hurrying toward the Algerian border. We crossed the chastened, dry-weather Oued Moulouya and the flat rich farmlands north of the Zegzel country where the Beni Snassen live. It was getting dark as we went through Berkane, new and resplendent. The town was full of people, palms and fluorescent lights. After Nador it looked like Hong Kong. But we decided not to stop, because we wanted to get to Oujda in time to have dinner at the hotel, – that is, if the hotel were still functioning.

About seven o'clock we saw the lights of Martimprey spread out ahead, perhaps twenty miles away, slightly below us. While we were still looking out across the plain, three flares exploded overhead and sailed slowly earthward. Very strong searchlight beams began to revolve, projected from behind the mountains in Algeria. There was a turn-off before Martimprey; we got onto the Saidia road just south of the town. That avoided possible difficulties with the authorities, for Martimprey is literally on the frontier, and is little more than a military headquarters these days. On this road there was a certain small amount of traffic. About every ten minutes we met a car coming toward us. Ahead there was a nervous driver who steadfastly refused to let us pass him. But when Christopher slowed down, in order to let him get well ahead of us, he slowed down too; there was no way of not being directly behind him. In exasperation Christopher finally drew up beside the road and stopped, saying: "I want to see a little of this war, anyway. Let's watch a while." The red flares illumined the mountainsides to the east, and the sharp beams of blue light intersected each other at varying angles. It was completely silent; there were not even any crickets. But the other car had stopped too, perhaps five hundred feet ahead of us, and soon we saw a figure approaching. Mohammed Larbi whispered: "If he asks questions, just answer them. He has a pistol." "How do you know?" I countered, but he did not reply. Christopher had turned off the headlights and the road was very dark, so we were not able to see his face until he had come right up to us.

"*Vous êtes en panne?*" he inquired, looking in through the front window like a customs inspector. In the reflection from the dashboard light I could see that he was young and well-dressed. He made a swift examination of the interior by turning his head slowly from one side to the other. The searchlights continued to move across the sky. We said we were only watching, as though we were in a shop where we didn't want to buy anything. "I see," he said presently. "I thought maybe you were in trouble." We thanked him. "Not at all," he said lightly, and he went back into the darkness. A minute or two later we heard the door of his car shut, but the motor did not start up. We waited another ten minutes or so; then Christopher turned on the headlights and the motor. The other car did likewise, started up, and kept ahead of us all the way to Oujda. Before we got to the centre it turned down a side-street and disappeared.

I had been afraid that with the Algerian border closed the *raison d'être* of the Hotel Terminus would be gone, and it might no longer exist. It is open as usual, but its prices are much higher and the food has deteriorated. What the food now lacks in quality the service compensates for in pretentiousness. Dinner was served outdoors under the palms, around a large circular basin of water. The popping of corks punctuated the sequences of French conversation. Suddenly there was a very loud explosion; the ground under my feet shuddered a little with the force of it. No one seemed to have noticed; the relaxed monotone of words and laughter continued as before. Within the minute there was another boom, somewhat less strong, but still powerful. When the waiter came up I questioned him.

"It's the bombardments in the Tlemcen sector," he said. "*Un engagement*. It's being going on for the past two nights. Sometimes it's quiet for a week or so, sometimes it's very active." During dessert there was a long string of machine-gun fire not more than half a mile distant – in Oujda itself. "What's that?" I demanded. The waiter's face did not change. "I didn't hear anything," he said. All kinds of things happen in Oujda nowadays, and no one asks any questions.

This was the night De Gaulle was to make his long-awaited "peace" offer to the F.L.N. via the radio. Out of idle curiosity, we went immediately upstairs after eating to listen to it. While the General intoned his pious-sounding syllables the deep-toned explosions continued outside, sometimes like nearby thunder and sometimes quite recognizably with the noise of bombs. Mohammed Larbi sat quietly, filling empty cigarette papers with kif and tamping them down before closing the ends. Now and then he demanded: "What's he saying?" (for he has never learned French), and each time he made the query I quickly said: "*Reh*." (Wind.) Christopher was annoyed with both of us. He has never been violently partisan in the Algerian dispute, because he is willing to credit the French with a modicum of good will. In order not to disturb his listening, I went to stand on the balcony, where I could hear the bombs instead of the words. There was no hypocrisy in their sound, no difference between what they meant and what they said, which was: death to Algerians. I wondered how many millions of Moslems in North Africa were hearing the radio words at that instant, and imagined the epithets of contempt and hatred coming from their lips as they listened. "*Zbil!*" "*Jiffa!*" "*Kharra!*" "*Ouild d'l qhaba!*" "*Inaal dinou!*" "*El khannez!*" When the General had finished his monologue, Christopher said sadly: "I only hope they believe him." I didn't think there was much danger of that, so I said nothing. The noise from the front kept going until a little after midnight. I felt feverish again, and I had to hunt for my clinical thermometer. It registered a little over 39 degrees. "Multiply by one point eight and add thirty-two. A hundred and two point two. My God! I'm sick."

"I've got to go to bed," I announced.

—Oujda
September 18

I stayed in bed yesterday morning. About three in the afternoon I got up long enough to drive to the Governor's office. He too was in Meknès with the Sultan, and his *katib* was politely unco-operative. His jurisdiction extended to the Beni Snassen, he agreed, but the truth was that the Beni Snassen had absolutely no music; in fact, he declared, they hire their musicians from the Beni Uriaghel when they need music. Nothing. And Figuig? I suggested. "There is no music in Figuig," he said flatly. "You can go. But you will get no music. I guarantee you that." I understood that he meant he would see to it that we got none. The anger was beginning to boil up inside me, and I thought it more prudent to get out of his office quickly. I thanked him and went back to bed. He is not an unusual type, the partially educated young Moroccan for whom material progress has become such an important symbol that he would be willing to sacrifice the religion, culture, happiness, and even the lives of his compatriots in order to achieve even a modicum of it. Few of them are as frank about their convictions as the official in Fez who told me: "I detest all folk music, and particularly ours here in Morocco. It sounds like the noises made by savages. Why should I help you to export a thing which we are trying to destroy? You are looking for tribal music. There are no more tribes. We have dissolved them. So the word means nothing. And there never was any tribal music anyway – only noise. *Non, monsieur*, I am not in accord with your project." In reality, the present government's policy is far less extreme than this man's opinion. The music itself has not been much tampered with – only the lyrics, which are now indoctrinated with patriotic sentiments. Practically all large official celebrations are attended by groups of folk musicians from all over the country; their travel and living expenses are paid by the government, and they perform before large audiences. As a result the performing style is becoming slick, and the extended forms are disappearing in favour of truncated versions which are devoid of musical sense.

—*Oujda*
September 20

I have lain in bed for the past three days, feverish and depressed, having lost the Beni Snassen as well as the others. Now all that remains open to me in the way of Riffian music is that of the

Gzennaia. They live in the Province of Taza, and it will probably be difficult to get to them because of the roads.

During the day there seems to be no sound from the front, but at night the bombardments begin, shortly after dark, and continue for three or four hours. Mohammed Larbi refuses to go out of the hotel: he claims Oujda is a dangerous place these days. According to him, there are ambushes and executions daily. I suspect that most of the explosions we hear during the day are fireworks celebrating the beginning of Mouloud, but I agree that some of the sounds are hard to explain away in that manner. In any case, the city is too close to the border to be restful. All I want is to be well enough to leave for Taza.

—Taza
September 22

Yesterday morning I had no fever at all, so in spite of feeling a little shaky, I got up and packed, and we set out on the road once more. It was a cool, sunny morning when we left. As we got into the desert beyond El Ayoun, however, the heat waves began to dance on the horizon. We ate in a wheatfield outside Taourirt. Passersby stopped under the tamarisk trees and sat down to watch us. When we got back into the car there was a struggle going on among several of them for possession of the empty tins and bottles we had left.

By the time we arrived in Taza, it was nearly sunset, and I was ready again for bed. But since the government buildings had not yet shut for the night I decided to try and see the Governor while I was still up and walking around. I had a feeling that the fever had returned. I went straight to the hotel from there to get into bed, and I have not yet got out of it, so it is just as well that I stayed up an extra hour and saw the *katib*. (The Governor, not surprisingly, was in Meknès with the Sultan.)

This *katib* was a young intellectual with thick-lensed glasses. He made it clear that he thought my project an absurdity, but he did not openly express disapproval. He even went through the motions of telephoning all the way to Aknoul to a surbordinate up there in the mountains.

"I see, I see," he said presently. "He died last year. Ah, yes. Too bad. And Ţizi Ouzli?" he added, as I gestured and stage-whispered to him. "Nothing there, either. I see." He listened a while, commenting in monosyllables from time to time, then finally thanked his informant and hung up.

"The last *chikh* in Aknoul died last summer. He was an old man. There is no music in the region. In Tizi Ouzli the people won't come out. When the Sultan went through, the women refused to leave their houses to sing for him. So you see . . . " He smiled, spreading his hands out, palms up. "it will not be possible with the Gzennaia."

I sat looking at him while he spoke, already aware of what he was going to report, letting fragments of thoughts flit through my tired head. "How they mistrust and fear the Riffians! But how naive this one is, to admit openly that the alienation is so great! Were the women punished? . . . " And I remembered a remark a Riffian had once made to me: "You have your Negroes in America, and Morocco has us."

"End of the Rif," I said sadly to Christopher.

The young *katib* pointed to the wall map behind his desk. "In the Middle Atlas, on the other hand, I can arrange something for you. Within a very few days, if you like. The Ait Ouaraine."

"Yes, I should like it very much," I told him.

"Come, please, tomorrow morning at ten o'clock."

"Thank you," we said.

I came back here to the Hôtel Guillaume Tell and got into bed. The room is not made up here, either, but there is plenty of space in it, and my meals are brought up on a tray, so it is not important. Yesterday Christopher and Mohammed Larbi made contact in the street with a group of professional musicians who agreed to record today. Their ensemble consisted of three *rhaitas*, four *tbola* (beaten with sticks) and eight rifles. The first price asked was high; then it was explained that if the rifles were not to be fired during the playing the cost would be cut in half. The agreement reached provided that only the *rhaitas* and *tbola* would perform.

Mohammed Larbi's excessive consumption of kif has given him a serious chronic liver disorder; he feels ill most of the time. Last night he went out for a walk after dinner. At the end of an hour he came in, his expression more determined than usual, and announced to us: "I'm finished with kif." Christopher laughed derisively. To implement his words, Mohammed Larbi tossed both his *naboula*, bulging with kif, and his cherished pipe, on my bed, saying: "Keep all this. You can have it. I don't want to see any of it again." But this morning before breakfast he went out and bought a fifth of Scotch, which he sampled before his morning coffee. When he came into my room later to pack up the equipment for recording, he had the bottle with him, and Christopher made loud fun of him.

"*O chnou brhitsi?*" he cried indignantly. "I'm not smoking kif any more. Do you expect me to leave my poor head *empty?*" This amused Christopher and depressed me. I foresee difficulties with a belligerent Mohammed Larbi. Kif keeps men quiet and vegetative; alcohol sends them out to break shop windows. In Mohammed Larbi's case it often means a fight with a policeman. I watched with misgivings as he prepared to go out.

This was the first time any recording had been done in my absence. But it all went smoothly, said Christopher on their return. There was a slight altercation at the moment of payment, because in spite of the agreement by which the men were not to discharge their rifles, they had not been able to resist participating, so that at three separate points in the music they fired them off, all eight of them, and simultaneously. At the end they presented a bill for twenty-four cartridges, which Mohammed Larbi, by then well fortified with White Label, steadfastly refused to pay. "All right. Good-bye," they said, and they went happily off to play at a wedding in a nearby village.

—Taza
September 22

The whiskey has done its work, but in a fashion I had not expected. This evening, when the bottle was nearly empty, Mohammed Larbi spent two hours trying to telephone his wife in Tangier. Finally he got the proprietor of a grocery near his house to go and fetch her, and had a stormy conversation with her for five minutes. I could hear him bellowing from where I lay, at the other end of the hotel. When he came into my room he looked maniacal.

"I've heard my wife's voice!" he shouted. "Now I've got to see her. She may have somebody else. I'm going tonight. I'll get there by tomorrow night."

"You're walking out on your job?"

"I'm going to see my *wife*!" he cried, even louder, as though I had not understood. "I *have* to do that, don't I?"

"You're going to leave me here, sick in bed?"

He hesitated only an instant. "Christopher knows how to take care of you. Besides, you're not sick. You just have a fever. I'll give you the grocer's number, and you telephone me when you get to Fez. I'll see you in a week or ten days, in Fez."

"All right," I said, without any intention of calling him. If he is going to be on whiskey, it would be better not to have him along, in any case.

And so now I have at least a pound of very strong kif among my possessions. In another two or three days I should be well enough to go up to Tahala and capture the Ait Ouaraine. The Rif is finished, and I managed to record only in two places.

BAPTISM OF SOLITUDE •

Immediately when you arrive in the Sahara, for the first or the tenth time, you notice the stillness. An incredible, absolute silence prevails outside the towns; and within, even in busy places like the markets, there is a hushed quality in the air, as if the quiet were a conscious force which, resenting the intrusion of sound, minimizes and disperses it straightaway. Then there is the sky, compared to which all other skies seem faint-hearted efforts. Solid and luminous, it is always the focal point of the landscape. At sunset, the precise, curved shadow of the earth rises into it swiftly from the horizon, cutting it into light section and dark section. When all daylight is gone, and the space is thick with stars, it is still of an intense and burning blue, darkest directly overhead and paling toward the earth, so that the night never really grows dark.

You leave the gate of the fort or the town behind, pass the camels lying outside, go up into the dunes, or out onto the hard, stony plain and stand a while, alone. Presently, you will either shiver and hurry back inside the walls, or you will go on standing there and let something very peculiar happen to you, something that everyone who lives there has undergone, and which the French call *le baptême de la solitude*. It is a unique sensation, and it has nothing to do with loneliness, for loneliness presupposes memory. Here, in this wholly mineral landscape lighted by stars like flares, even memory disappears; nothing is left but your own breathing and the sound of your heart beating. A strange, and by no means pleasant, process of reintegration begins inside you, and it remains to be seen whether you will fight against it, and insist on remaining the person you have always been, or whether you will let it take its course. For no one who has stayed in the Sahara for a while is quite the same as when he came.

Before the war for independence in Algeria, under the rule of the French military, there was a remarkable feeling of friendly sympathy among Europeans in the Sahara. It is unnecessary to stress the fact that the corollary of this pleasant state of affairs was the exercise of the strictest sort of colonial control over the Algerians themselves, a regime which amounted to a reign of terror. But from the European viewpoint the place was ideal. The whole vast region was like a small unspoiled rural community where everyone respected the rights of everyone else. Each time you lived there for a while, and left it, you were struck with the indifference and the impersonality of the world outside. If during your travels there, you forgot something, you could be sure of finding it later on your way back; the idea of appropriating it would not have occurred to anyone. You could wander where you liked, out in the wilderness or in the darkest alleys of the towns; no one would molest you.

At that time, no members of the indigent, wandering, unwanted proletariat from northern Algeria had come down here, because there was nothing to attract them. Almost everyone owned a parcel of land in an oasis and lived by working it. In the shade of the date palms, wheat, barley and corn were grown, and those plants provided the staple items of diet. There were usually two or three Arab or Negro shopkeepers who sold things like sugar, tea, candles, matches, carbide for lighting, and cheap European cotton goods. In the larger towns there was sometimes a shop kept by a European, but the merchandise was the same, because the customers were virtually all natives. Almost without exception, the only Europeans who lived in the Sahara were the military and the ecclesiastic.

As a rule, the military and their aides were friendly men, agreeable to be with, interested in showing visitors everything worth seeing in their districts. This was fortunate, as the traveller was often completely at their mercy. He might have to depend on them for his food and lodging, since in the smaller places there were no hotels. Generally he had to depend on them for contact with the outside world, because anything he wanted, like cigarettes or wine, had to be brought by truck from the military post, and his mail was sent in care of the post, too. Furthermore, the decision as to whether he was to have permission to move about freely in the region rested with the military. The power to grant those privileges was vested in, let us say, one lonely lieutenant who lived two hundred miles from his nearest countryman, ate badly, (anathema to any Frenchman) and wished that neither camels, date-palms, nor inquisitive foreigners had ever been created. Still, it was rare to find an indifferent or unhelpful commandant. He was likely to invite you for drinks and dinner, show you the curiosities he had collected during his years in the bled, ask you to accompany him on his tours of inspection, or even to spend a fortnight with him and his *peloton* of several dozen native *meharistes* when they went out into the desert to make topographical surveys. Then you would be given your own camel – not an ambling pack camel that had to be driven with a stick by someone walking beside it, but a swift, trained animal that obeyed the slightest tug of the reins.

More extraordinary were the Pères Blancs, intelligent and well-educated. There was no element of resignation in their eagerness to spend the remainder of their lives in distant outposts, dressed as Moslems, speaking Arabic, living in the rigorous, comfortless manner of the desert inhabitants. They made no converts, and expected to make none. "We are here only to show the Moslem that the Christian can be worthy of respect," they would explain. One used to hear the Moslems say that although the Christians might be masters of the earth, the Moslems were the masters of Heaven; for the military it was quite enough that the "indigène" recognize European supremacy here. Obviously the White Fathers could not be satisfied with that. They insisted upon proving to the inhabitants that the Nazarene was capable of leading as exemplary a life as the most ardent follower of Mohammed. It is true that the austerity of the Fathers' mode of life inspired many Moslems with respect for them, if not for the civilization they represented. And as a result of the years spent in the desert among the inhabitants, the Fathers acquired a certain healthy and unorthodox fatalism, an excellent adjunct to their spiritual equipment, and a highly necessary one in dealing with the men among whom they had chosen to live.

With an area considerably larger than that of the United States, the Sahara is a continent within a continent – a skeleton, if you like, but still a separate entity from the rest of Africa which surrounds it. It has its own mountain ranges, rivers, lakes and forests, but they are largely vestigial. The mountain ranges have been reduced to gigantic bouldery bumps that rise above the neighbouring countryside like the mountains on the moon. Some of the rivers appear as such for perhaps one day a year – others much less often. The lakes are of solid salt, and the forests have long since petrified. But the physical contours of the landscape vary as much as they do anywhere else. There are plains, hills, valleys, gorges, rolling lands, rocky peaks and volcanic craters, all without vegetation or even soil. Yet, probably the only parts that are monotonous to the eye are regions like the Tanezrouft, south of Reggan, a stretch of about five hundred miles of absolutely flat, gravel-strewn terrain, without the slightest sign of life, nor the smallest undulation in the land, to vary the implacable line of the horizon on all sides. After being here for a while, the sight of even a rock awakens an emotion in the traveller; he feels like crying: "Land!"

There is no known historical period when the Sahara has not been inhabited by man. Most of the other larger forms of animal life, whose abode it formerly was, have become extinct. If we believe the evidence of cave drawings, we can be sure that the giraffe, the hippopotamus and the rhinoceros were once dwellers in the region. The lion has disappeared from North Africa in our own time, likewise the ostrich. Now and then a crocodile is still discovered in some distant, hidden oasis pool, but the occurrence is so rare that when it happens it is a great event. The camel, of course, is not a native of Africa at all, but an importation from Asia, having arrived approximately at the time of the end of the Roman Empire – about when the last elephants were killed off. Large numbers of the herds of wild elephants that roamed the northern reaches of the desert were captured and trained for use in the Carthaginian army, but it was the Romans who finally annihilated the species to supply ivory for the European market.

Fortunately for man, who seems to insist on continuing to live in surroundings which become increasingly inhospitable to him, gazelles are still plentiful, and there are, paradoxically enough, various kinds of edible fish in the water holes – often more than a hundred feet deep – throughout the Sahara. Certain species which abound in artesian wells are blind, having always lived deep in the subterranean lakes.

An often-repeated statement, no matter how incorrect, takes a long time to disappear from circulation. Thus, there is a popular misconception of the Sahara as a vast region of sand across which Arabs travel in orderly caravans from one white-domed city to another, and it still prevails. A generalization much nearer to the truth would be to say that it is an area of rugged mountains, bare valleys and flat, stony wasteland, sparsely dotted with Negro villages of mud. The sand in the Sahara, according to data supplied by the Geographical Service of the French Army, covers only about a tenth of its surface, and the Arabs, most of whom are nomads, form a small part of the population. The vast majority of the inhabitants are of Berber (native North African) and/or Negro (native West African) stock. But the Negroes of today are not those who originally peopled the desert. The latter never took kindly to the colonial designs of the Arabs and the Islamised Berbers who collaborated with them; over the centuries they beat a constant retreat toward the southeast until only a vestige of their society remains, in the region now known as the Tibesti. They were replaced by the more docile Sudanese, imported from the south as slaves to work the constantly expanding series of oases.

In the Sahara the oasis – which is to say, the forest of date palms – is primarily a man-made affair, and can continue its existence only if the work of irrigating its terrain is kept up unrelentingly. When the Arabs arrived in Africa twelve centuries ago, they began a project of land reclamation which, if the Europeans continue it with the aid of modern machinery, will transform much of the Sahara into a great, fertile garden. Wherever there was a sign of vegetation, the water was there not far below; it merely needed to be brought to the surface. The Arabs set to work digging wells, constructing reservoirs, building networks of canals along the surface of the ground and systems of subterranean water-galleries deep in the earth.

For all these important projects, the recently arrived colonizers needed great numbers of workers who could bear the climate and the malaria that is still endemic in the oases. Sudanese slaves seemed to be the ideal solution of the problem, and these came to constitute the larger part of the sedentary population of the desert. Each Arab tribe travelled about among the oases it controlled, collecting the produce. It was never the practice or the intention of the sons of Allah to live there. They have a saying which goes: "No one lives in the Sahara if he is able to live anywhere else". Slavery has, of course, been abolished officially by the French, but only recently, within our time. Probably the principal factor in the process by which Timbuctoo was reduced from its status of capital of the Sahara to its present abject condition was the closing of the slave market there. But the Sahara, which started out as a Negro country, is still a Negro country, and will undoubtedly remain so for a long time.

The oases, those magnificent palm groves, are the blood and bone of the desert; life in the Sahara would be unthinkable without them. Wherever human beings are found, an oasis is sure to be nearby. Sometimes the town is surrounded by the trees, but usually it is built just outside, so that none of the fertile ground will be wasted on mere living- quarters. The size of an oasis is reckoned by the number of trees it contains, not by the number of square miles it covers, just as the taxes are based on the number of date-bearing trees, and not on the amount of land. The prosperity of a region is in direct proportion to the number and size of its oases. The one at Figuig, for instance, has more than two hundred thousand bearing palms, and the one at Timimoun is forty miles long, with irrigation systems that are of an astonishing complexity.

To stroll in a Saharan oasis is rather like taking a walk through a well-kept Eden. The alleys are clean, bordered on each side by hand-patted mud walls, not too high to prevent you from seeing the riot of verdure within. Under the high waving palms are the smaller trees – pomegranate, orange, fig, almond. Below these, in neat squares surrounded by narrow ditches of running water, are the vegetables and wheat. No matter how far from the town you stray, you have the same impression of order, cleanliness, and insistence on utilizing every square inch of ground. When you come to the edge of the oasis, you always find that it is in the process of being enlarged. Plots of young palms extend out into the glaring wasteland. Thus far they are useless, but in a few years they will begin to bear, and eventually this sun-blistered land will be a part of the green belt of gardens.

There are a good many birds living in the oases, but their songs and plumage are not appreciated by the inhabitants. The birds eat the young shoots and dig up the seeds as fast as they are planted, and practically every man and boy carries a slingshot. A few years ago I travelled through the Sahara with a parrot; everywhere the poor bird was glowered at by the natives, and in Timimoun a delegation of three elderly men came to the hotel one afternoon and suggested that I stop leaving its cage in the window; otherwise there was no telling what its fate might be. "Nobody likes birds here." they said meaningfully.

It is the custom to build little summer-houses out in the oasis. There is often an element of play and fantasy in the architecture of these edifices which makes them captivating. They are small, toy palaces of mud. Here, men have tea with their families at the close of day, or spend the night when it is unusually hot in the town, or invite their friends for a game of *ronda* and a little music. If a man asks you to visit him in his summer-house, you find that the experience is invariably worth the long walk required to get there. You will have to drink at least the three traditional glasses of tea, and you may have to eat a good many almonds and smoke more kif than you really want, but it will be cool, there will be the gurgle of running water and the smell of mint in the air, and your host may bring out a flute. One winter I priced one of these houses that had particularly struck my fancy. With its garden and pool, the cost was the equivalent of twenty-five pounds. The catch was that the owner wanted to retain the right to work the land, because it was unthinkable to him that it should cease to be productive.

Even though people of dissimilar origins may behave alike in every-day life, the differences become apparent in festive observ- ances. In the highly religious settlement of the M'Zab, it would be inconceivable for the women to take part in a celebration; they stay on the roofs where Moslem women belong. From here they scream exhortations to the men who are below in the street, under- going the frenetic, self-immolating contortions of their dance. I once spent a night in Ghardaia watching a dozen men dance themselves into unconsciousness beside a bonfire of palm branches. Two burly guards were necessary to prevent them from throwing themselves into the flames. After each man had been heaved back from the fire several times, he finally ceased making his fantastic skyward leaps, staggered, and sank to the ground. He was immediate- ly carried outside the circle and covered with blankets, his place being taken by a fresh adept. There was no music or singing, but there were eight drummers, each playing an instrument of a different size.

In other places, the dance is similar to the Berber *ahouache* of the Moroccan Atlas. The participants form a great circle holding hands, women alternating with men; their movements are measured, never frantic, and, although the trance is constantly suggested, it seems never to be arrived at collectively. In the performances I have seen, there has been a woman in the centre with her head and neck hidden by a cloth. She sings and dances, and the chorus around her responds antiphonally. It is all very sedate and low- pitched, but the irrational seems never very far away, perhaps because of the hypnotic effect produced by the slowly beaten, deep-toned drums.

The Touareg, in all probability an ancient offshoot of the Kabyle Berbers of Algeria, were unappreciative of the "civilizing mission" of the Roman legions, and decided to put a thousand miles or more of desert between themselves and their would-be educators. They went straight south until they came to a land that seemed likely to provide them the privacy they desired, and they have remained throughout the centuries, their own masters almost until today. Through all the ages during which the Arabs dominated the surrounding regions, the Touareg retained their rule of the Hoggar, that immense plateau in the very centre of the Sahara. Their traditional hatred of the Arabs, however, does not appear to have been powerful enough to keep them from becoming partially Islamised, although they are by no means a completely Moslem people. Far from being a piece of property only somewhat more valuable than a sheep, the woman has an extremely important place in Targui society. The line of succession is purely maternal. Here, it is the men who must be veiled day and night. The veil is of fine black gauze, and is worn, so they explain, to protect the soul. But since soul and breath to them are identical, it is not difficult to find a physical reason, if one is desired. The excessive dryness of the atmosphere often causes disturbances in the nasal passages. The veil conserves the breath's mosture, is a sort of little air-conditioning plant, and this helps to keep out the evil spirits which otherwise would manifest their presence by making the nostrils bleed, a common occurrence in this part of the world.

It is scarcely fair to refer to these proud people as Touareg. The word is a term of opprobrium meaning "lost souls", given them by their traditional enemies the Arabs, but one which, in the outside world, has stuck. They call themselves *imochagh*, the free ones. Among all the Berber-speaking peoples, they are the only ones to have devised a system of writing their language. No one knows how long their alphabet has been in use, but it is a true phonetical alphabet, quite as well planned and logical as the Roman one, with twenty-three simple and thirteen compound letters.

Unfortunately for them the Touareg have never been able to remain at peace among themselves; internecine warfare has gone on unceasingly among them for centuries. Until the French military put a stop to it, it had been a common practice for one tribe to set out on plundering expeditions against a neighbouring tribe. During these voyages, the wives of the absent men remained faithful to their husbands, the strict Targui moral code recommending death as a punishment for infidelity. However, a married woman whose husband was away was free to go at night to the graveyard dressed in her finest apparel, lie on the tombstone of one of her ancestors, and invoke a certain spirit called Idebni, who always appeared in the guise of one of the young men of the community. If she could win Idebni's favour, he gave her news of her husband; if not, he strangled her. The Touareg women, being very clever, always managed to bring back news of their husbands from the cemetery.

The first motor crossing of the Sahara was accomplished in 1923. At that time it was still a matter of months to get from, let us say, Touggourt to Zinder, or from the Tafilalet to Gao. In 1934, I was in Erfoud inquiring about caravans to Timbuctoo. Yes, they said, one was leaving in a few weeks; and it would take from sixteen to twenty weeks to make the voyage. How would I get back? The caravan would probably set out on its return trip at this time next year. They were surprised to see that this information lessened my interest. How could you expect to do it more quickly?

Of course, the proper way to travel in the Sahara is by camel, particularly if you are a good walker, since after about two hours of the camel's motion you are glad to get down and walk for four. Each succeeding day is likely to bring with it a greater percentage of time spent off the camel. Nowadays, if you like, you can leave Algiers in the morning by plane, and be fairly well into the desert by evening, but the traveller who gives in to this temptation, like the reader of a mystery story who skips through the book to arrive at the solution quickly, deprives himself of most of the pleasure of the journey. The practical means of locomotion here today for the person who wants to see something, is the trans-Saharan truck, a compromise between camel and aeroplane.

There are only two trails across the desert at present (the Piste Impériale through Mauretania not being open to the public) and I should not recommend either to drivers of private automobiles. The trucks, however, are especially built for the region. If there is any sort of misadventure, the wait is not likely to be more than twenty-four hours, since the truck is always expected at the next town, and there is always an ample supply of water aboard. But the lone car that gets stuck in the Sahara is in trouble.

Usually, you can go to the fort of any town and telephone ahead to the next post, asking them to notify the hotelkeeper there of your intended arrival. Should the lines be down, a not unusual circumstance, there is no way of assuring yourself a room in advance, save by mail, which is extremely slow. Unless you travel with your own blankets this can be a serious drawback, arriving unannounced, for the hotels are small, often having only five or six rooms, and the winter nights are cold. The temperature goes to several degrees below freezing, reaching its lowest point just before dawn. The same courtyard that may show 125 when it is flooded with sun at two in the afternoon will register only 28 the following morning. So it is good to know you are going to have a room and a bed in your next stopping place. Not that there is heating of any sort in the establishments, but by keeping the window shut you can help the thick mud walls conserve some of the daytime heat. Even so, I have awakened to find a sheet of ice over the water in the glass beside my bed.

These violent extremes of temperatures are due, of course, to the dryness of the atmosphere, whose relative humidity is often less than five percent. When you reflect that the soil attains a temperature of 175° during the summer, you understand that the principal consideration in planning streets and houses should be that of keeping out as much light as possible. The streets are kept dark by building them underneath and inside the houses, and the houses have no windows in their massive walls. The French have introduced the window into much of their architecture, but their windows open onto wide, vaulted arcades, and thus, while they do give air, they let in little light. The result is that once you are out of the sun you live in a Stygian gloom.

Even in the Sahara there is no spot where rain has not been known to fall, and its arrival is an event that calls for celebration — drumming, dancing, firing of guns. The storms are violent and unpredictable. Considering their disastrous effects, one wonders that the people can welcome them with such unmixed emotions. Enormous walls of water rush down the dry river beds, pushing everything before them, isolating the towns. The roofs of the houses cave in, and often the walls themselves. A prolonged rain would destroy every town in the Sahara, since the *tob*, of which everything is built, is softer than our adobe. And, in fact, it is not unusual to see a whole section of a village which has been forsaken by its occupants, who have rebuilt their houses nearby, leaving the walls and foundations of their former dwellings to dissolve and drop back into the earth of which they were made.

In 1932 I decided to spend the winter in the M'Zab of southern Algeria. The rattletrap bus started out from Laghouat at night in a heavy rain. Not far to the south, the trail crossed a flat stretch about a mile wide, slightly lower than the surrounding country. Even as we were in it, the water began to rise around us, and in a moment the motor died. The passengers jumped out and waded about in water that soon was up to their waists; in all directions there were dim white figures in burnouses moving slowly through the flood, like storks. They were looking for a shallow route back to dry land, but they did not find it. In the end they carried me, the only European in the party, all the way to Laghouat on their backs, leaving the bus and its luggage to drown out there in the rain. When I got to Ghardaia two days later, the rain (which was the first in seven years) had made a deep pond beside an embankment the French had built for the trail. Such an enormous quantity of water all in one place was a source of great excitement to the inhabitants. For days there was a constant procession of women coming to carry it away in jugs. The children tried to walk on its surface, and two small ones were drowned. Ten days later the water had almost disappeared. A thick, brilliant green froth covered what was left, but the women continued to come with their jugs. pushing aside the scum and taking what remained. For once, they were able to collect as much water as they could store in their houses. Ordinarily, it was an expensive commodity that they had to buy each morning from the town watersellers, who brought it in from the oasis.

Most of the towns are better supplied with water than Ghardaia was then. But the quality of the water varies greatly, and the traveller does well to look into the matter at each place before drinking it. It is better to know whether the minerals it contains are likely to cause death, illness, or merely acute alimentary disturbances. But it is not bad water so much as no water that one had to fear. It is impossible to have too much of it with you. People still die regularly of thirst in the Sahara, so one should take along, on every stage of the journey, more than one can imagine will be needed. Then, if strange explosions and groans are heard among the rocks, the traveller will be aware that it is only a result of the sudden shifts in temperature, and not the laughter of el Rhoul, the *djinn* who comes to watch the thirsty traveller in his death agonies.

There are probably few accessible places on the face of the globe where you can get less comfort for your money than the Sahara. In the past few years the prices in dollars or sterling have more than quintupled, and the accomodations are as miserable as ever. You can still get something flat to lie down on, stewed turnips and sand, noodles and jam, and a few tendons of something euphemistically called chicken to eat, and the stub of a candle to undress by at night, but you will pay heavily for these luxuries. Inasmuch as you must carry your own food and stove with you in any case, it sometimes seems scarcely worthwhile to bother with the "meals" provided by the hotels. But if you depend entirely on your tinned goods, they give out too quickly. Everything disappears eventually anyway – your coffee, tea, sugar, cigarettes – and you settle down to a life devoid of these superfluities, using a pile of soiled clothing as a pillow for your head at night and your burnous for a blanket.

Perhaps the logical question to ask at this point is: Why go? The answer is that once you have been there and undergone the baptism of solitude you cannot help yourself. Once you have been under the spell of the vast, luminous, silent country, no other place is quite strong enough, no other surroundings can provide the supremely satisfying sensation of existing in the midst of something that is absolute. The traveller will return, whatever the cost in comfort and money, for the absolute has no price.

THE ROUTE TO TASSEMSIT •

Whenever I leave Tangier to go south, my home takes on the look of a place where serious disaster has just struck. The night before I set out on this particular trip, the usual disorder prevailed. There were crates of canned foodstuffs and bundles of blankets and pillows in the living room. The recording equipment was scattered over an unnecessarily large area, so that coils of extra cable hid the portable butane-gas stove and boxes of tape covered the road maps. The servants had induced me to write down the specifications of the things they hoped I would remember to buy for them while I was there. Fatima wanted a white woollen blanket at least eight meters long, and Mina a silver-plated circular tray with three detachable legs. Following tradition, they had scrupulously insisted that these things were to be paid for out of their wages after I returned, and I had agreed, although each of us was aware that such deductions would never be made. Moroccan etiquette demands that when the master of the house goes on a journey he bring back souvenirs for everyone. The farther he goes and the longer he stays, the more substantial these gifts are expected to be.

In this country departure is often a pre-dawn activity. After the half-hour of early morning prayer-calling is finished and the muezzins have extinguished the lights at the tops of the minarets, there is still about an hour of dark left. The choir of roosters trails on in the air above the rooftops of the city until daybreak. It is a good moment to leave, just as the sky is growing white in the east and objects are black and sharp against it. By the time the sun was up, Christopher and I were far out in the country, rolling along at a speed determined only by the curves and the occasional livestock in the road. The empty highway, visible far ahead, measured off the miles of grandiose countryside, and along the way no billboards came between us and the land.

During the last six months of 1959 I travelled some twenty-five thousand miles around Morocco, recording music for the

Library of Congress on a grant from the Rockefeller Foundation. The quality of the material was uniformly splendid; nevertheless, one always has preferences. After a great deal of listening, the tapes which interested me most were the ones I had recorded in Tafraout, a region in the western Anti-Atlas. Since I had managed to get only six selections there, I wanted now to go back and try to find some more, although this time it would have to be without the assistance of the Moroccan Government. By my inland itinerary there was a distance of 1,370 kilometres (855 miles) to be covered between Tangier and Tafraout, and the roads would be fairly good all the way. The direct route to Marrakech via Rabat runs over flat terrain and has a certain amount of traffic along it. The unfrequented interior route we used, which leads through the western foothills of the Rif Mountains and over the Middle Atlas, takes an extra day, but is beautiful at every point.

Beyond Xauen we followed the River Loukos for a while, here a clear swift stream at the bottom of a narrow valley. Christopher, who was driving, suggested that it was time for lunch. We stopped, spread a rug under an old olive tree and ate, listening to the sound of the water skipping over the stones beside us. The hills rose steeply on both sides of the river. Not a person or a dwelling in sight. We started out again. A half-hour further on, we rounded a corner and came upon a man lying face down on the paved surface of the road, his djellaba covering his head. Immediately I thought: "He's dead". We stopped, got out, prodded him a bit, and he sat up, rubbing his eyes, mumbling, annoyed at being awakened. He explained that the clean, smooth road was a better place to sleep than the stony ground beside it. When we objected that he might easily be killed, he replied with fine peasant logic that no one had killed him yet. Nevertheless, he got up and walked a few yards off the highway, where he slumped down again all in one motion, wrapped the hood of his djellaba around his head, and went back into the comfortable world of sleep.

The next day was hotter. We climbed up along the slowly rising ramp of the Middle Atlas, a gray, glistening landscape. The shiny leaves of the scrub live-oaks, and even the exposed bedrock beneath, reflected the hot light of the overhead sun. Further along, on the southern slope of the mountains, we passed the mangled body of a large ape that had not got out of the road fast enough – an unusual sight here, since the monkeys generally stay far from the highways.

All afternoon we had been speeding along the gradually descending valley between the Middle Atlas and the Grand Atlas. The sun went down ahead of us and the moon rose behind us. We drank coffee from the thermos and hoped we would get into Marrakech in time to find some food. The new Moroccan regime has brought early closing hours to a land where heretofore night was merely a continuation of day.

After the lunar brightness of the empty waste-land, the oasis was dark. The highway went for miles between high mud walls and canebrakes; the black tracery of date-palms rose above them, against the brilliant night sky. Suddenly the walls and the oasis came to an end, and ahead, standing in the rubble of the desert, was a big new cinema trimmed with tubes of coloured neon, the tin and straw shacks of a *bidonville* clustering around it like the cottages of a village around the church. In Morocco the very poor live neither in the country nor in the city: they come as far as the outer walls of the town, build these desperate-looking squatters' colonies out of whatever materials they can find, and there they stay.

Marrakech is a city of great distances, flat as a table. When the wind blows, the pink dust of the plain sweeps into the sky, obscuring the sun, and the whole city, painted with a wash made of the pink earth on which it rests, glows red in the cataclysmic light. At night, from a car window, it looks not unlike one of our own Western cities: long miles of streetlights stretching in straight lines across the plain. Only by day does one see that most of these lights illumine nothing more than empty reaches of palm and desert. Over the years, the outer fringes of the Medina have been made navigable to automobiles and horse-drawn carriages, of which there are still a great many, but it takes a brave man to drive his car into the maze of serpentine alleys full of porters, bicycles, carts, donkeys and ordinary pedestrians. Besides, the only way to see anything in the Medina is to walk. In order to be really present, you must have your feet in the dust, and be aware of the hot dusty smell of the mud walls beside your face.

The night we arrived in Marrakech, Christopher and I went to a café in the heart of the Medina. On the roof under the stars they spread matting, blankets and cushions for us, and we sat there drinking mint tea, savouring the cool air that begins to stir above the city after midnight, when the stored heat of the sun is finally dissipated. At a certain moment, out of the silence of the street below, there came a succession of strange, explosive cries. I leaned over the edge and peered down into the dim passageway three floors beneath. Among the few late strollers an impossible, phantom-like figure was dancing. It galloped, it stopped, it made great gravitation-defying leaps into the air as if the earth under its feet were helping. At each leap it yelled. No one paid any attention. As the figure came along below the café, I was able to identify it as a powerfully built young man; he was almost naked. I watched him disappear into the dark. Almost immediately he returned, doing the same inspired dance, occasionally rushing savagely toward other pedestrians, but always stopping himself in time to be able to avoid touching them. He passed back and forth through the alley in this way for a quarter of an hour or so before the qahouaji climbed the ladder again to the roof where we sat. When he came I said casually: "What's going on down there?" Although in most places it would have been clear enough that a madman was loose in the streets, in Morocco there are subtle distinctions to be made. Sometimes the person turns out to be merely holy, or indisposed.

"Ah, poor man," said the qahouaji, "He's a friend of mine. We were in school together. He got high marks and played good soccer."

"What happened?"

"What do you think? A woman, of course."

This had not occurred to me. "You mean she worked magic on him?"

"What else? At first he was like this – " He let his jaw drop and his mouth hang open; his eyes became fixed and vacant. "Then after a few weeks he tore off his clothes and began to run. And ever since, he runs like that, in the summer and in the winter. The woman was rich. Her husband had died and she wanted Allal. But he's of a good family and they didn't like her. So she said in her head: 'No other woman is going to have him either.' And she gave him what she gave him."

"And his family?"

"He doesn't know his family. He lives in the street".

"And the woman? What happened to her?"

He shrugged. "She's not here any more. She moved somewhere else". At that moment the cries came up again.

"But why do they let him run in the street like that? Can't they do anything for him?"

"Oh, he never hurts anybody. He's just playful. He likes to scare people, that's all".

I decided to put my question. "Is he crazy?"

"No, just playful".

"Ah, yes. I see".

At twilight one day we were the tea guests of Moulay Brahim, one of the Moroccans who previously had helped me make contacts with musicians. He lived in a rooming house near the dyers' souk. The establishment, on the second floor, consisted of a dozen or more cubicles situated around an open central court with a dead fountain in the middle. No women were allowed in the building; it was a place for men who have left home and family behind. Not an object was visible that could even remind one of the existence of traditional Moroccan life. Moulay Brahim is militantly of his epoch; his life is almost wholly abstract. He spends his hours in an attitude of prostration on his mattress, his head touching a large short-wave radio. He knows what time it is in Jakarta, just where the Nigerian representative to the United Nations is at this moment, and what Sékou Touré said to Nkrumah about Nasser. The radio is never silent save for a useless five minutes now and then while he waits impatiently for a programme in Cairo or Damascus or Baghdad to begin. He follows the moves in the cold war like an onlooker at a chess match, making searing comments on what he considers the blunders of both sides. Only the neutralist powers have his sympathy. We sat in the dusk around the dimly illumined radio and listened to it hiss and crackle. Moulay Brahim dispensed kif silently, intent on the panel of the instrument, weighing each gradation of static with the expression of a connoisseur certain of his ground. Fifteen minutes might go by without a trace of any sort of programme coming out – only the unvarying noise of interference. His face did not change; he knows how to wait. At any moment he may hear something more, something identifiable. Then he can relax for a bit, while the tea-concession man from across the courtyard brings in the big tray, sets up the glasses, and rolls the mint between his hands before stuffing it into the pot. But soon it is not enough for Moulay Brahim to know that he is in touch with the BBC service to the Middle East, and he begins once again the painful search for the unfindable. Inhabitants of the other rooms came in and squatted, but it was difficult to engage them in anything more than desultory conversaion. They had learned from experience that in Moulay Brahim's room it was better to be quiet. At one point when a particularly confused noise had for some time been issuing from the loudspeaker, I rashly suggested that he adjust the dial. "No, no!" he cried. "This is what I want. I've got five stations here now. Sometimes others come in. It's a place where they all like to get together and talk at once. Like in a café." For the young and deracinated Moroccan like Moulay Brahim, radio is primarily neither a form of entertainment nor a medium of information. It is a sort of metaphysical umbilical cord – a whole manner of existence, an essential adjunct to feeling that he is in contact with life.

When we had finally persuaded him that it was time for us to leave, he reluctantly rose from the radio and took us out into the streets to the apothecary market, where I had expressed a desire to go. It is the place you visit if you want the ingredients for making black magic. There were six stalls in a row, all bristling with the dried parts of birds, reptiles and mammals. We wandered slowly by, examining the horns, quills, hair, eggs, bones, feathers, feet and bills that were strung on wires in the doorways. I was put in mind of the unfortunate Allal and the rich widow, and I described Allal to Moulay Brahim. He knew him; everybody in Marrakech knew him, he declared, adding as he pointed to the rows of glass containers in front of us: "You can get everything for that sort of business here. But you've got to know how to blend them. That takes an expert." He raised his eyebrows significantly, and approached the nearest merchant to mutter a few words to him. A packet containing tiny seeds was brought out. Moulay Brahim examined them at some length, and bought fifty grams. "What is it?" I asked him. But he was enjoying his brief role as mystery man, and merely rattled the seeds in their paper, saying: "Something very special, very special."

*

Taroudant, Thursday 6th. – Brilliant day. Sky like a blue enamel bowl overhead. Left Marrakech at noon, driving straight up to Ouirgane, in a valley only about three thousand feet above the plain. Lunch outside in the sun at *Le Sanglier Qui Fume*. Our table midway between a chained eagle and a chained monkey, both of which watched us distrustfully while we ate. Below, hidden, somewhere nearby, the little river roared over its rocks. The Grand Atlas sun fiery. Monsieur gave us drooping old straw sombreros to wear while we ate. A tame stork, very proprietary, strutted around, poking its beak into everything. It was wary, however, of the monkey, which had a long bamboo pole in its hand and patiently tried to trip it up each time it came past. Everything excellent; hors d'oeuvre, frogs' legs and chicken paprika. Madame is Hungarian, said she lives in the hope that people coming through Ouirgane will prove to speak her language, " . . . or at least know Budapest," she added. Obviously disappointed in us. On up to the pass at Tizi n'Test and over the top. The valley of the Souss thick with a mist that looked like smoke. Only the long sloping rim of the Anti Atlas showed in the sky to the south, fifty miles across. Below, a gulf of vapour. Got into Taroudant at seven. The heat was still everywhere inside the walls. While I was unpacking, a procession of Guennaoua shuffled by in the street. Tried to get out through a door in the patio, but it was padlocked. I peeked through a crack and saw them going past slowly, carrying candle lanterns. The pounding of the drums shook the air.

*

After Taroudant, Tiznit, Tanout, Tirmi, Tiffermit. Great hot dust-coloured valleys among the naked mountains, dotted with leafless argan trees as grey as puffs of smoke. Sometimes a dry stream twists among the boulders at the bottom of a valley, and there is a peppering of locust-ravaged date palms whose branches look like the ribs of a broken umbrella. Or hanging to the flank of a mountain a thousand feet below the road is a terraced village, visible only as an abstract design of flat roofs, some the colour of the earth of which they are built, and some bright yellow with the corn that is spread out to dry in the sun.

The argan trees are everywhere, thousands of them, squat and thorny, anchored to the rocks that lie beneath in their dubious shade. They flourish where nothing else can live, not even weeds or cacti. Their scaly bark looks like crocodile hide and feels like iron. Where the argan grows the goats have a good life. The trunk is short and the branches begin to proliferate only a few feet from the ground. This suits the goats perfectly; they climb from branch to branch eating both the leaves and the greasy, bitter, olive-like fruit. Subsequently their excrement is collected, and the argan-pits in it are pressed to make a thick cooking oil.

Tafraout is rough country – the Bad Lands of south Dakota on a grand scale, with Death Valley in the background. The mountains are vast humps of solid granite, their sides strewn with gigantic boulders; at sunset the black line of their crests is deckle-edged in silhouette against the flaming sky. Seen from a height, the troughs between the humps are like long gray lakes, the only places in the landscape where there is at least a covering of what might pass for loose earth. Above the level surface of this detritus in the valleys rise the smooth expanses of solid rock.

The locusts have fed well here, too. Tafraout could never subsist on its dates. But the bourgeois Berbers who live here learned long ago that organized commerce could provide greater security than either the pastoral or the agricultural life. They inaugurated a successful campaign to create a virtual monopoly on grocery and hardware stores all over Morocco. Taking his male children with him, a man goes to a city in the north where he has a shop (or several shops) and remains there for two or three years at a stretch, usually living in conditions of extreme discomfort on the floor behind the counter. Being industrious, thrifty and invariably successful, he is naturally open to a good deal of adverse criticism from those of his compatriots who are less so, and who despise his frugal manner of living and deride his custom of leaving small boys of eight in charge of his shops. But the children run the establishments quite as well as their elders: they know the price of every object and are equally difficult to deal with in the national pastime of persuading the seller to lower his asking price. The boys merely refuse to talk; often they do not even look at the customer. They quote the price, and if it is accepted, hand over the article and return the change. It is a very serious matter to be in charge of a store, and the boys behave accordingly.

As you come up from Tiznit over the pass, the first Tafraout settlements on the trail occur at the neck of a narrow valley; built in among, underneath, and on top of the great fallen lumps of granite, the fortress-houses dominate the countryside. It is hard to reconcile the architectural sophistication of these pink and white castles with the unassuming aspect of their owners back in the north, just as it is difficult to believe that the splendid women, shrouded in black and carrying copper amphoras or calfskin-covered baskets on their shoulders, can be these inconspicuous little men's wives and sisters. But then, no one would expect a tribe of shopkeepers to have originated in the fastnesses of this savage landscape.

*

Tafraout, Sunday 9th. – Arrived yesterday about five after having a puncture ten miles up the trail. Hotel completely empty, save for a handful of ragged children and one old gentleman in a djellaba who has been left in charge of the premises while the regular guardian is down in Tiznit. He helped with luggage, hung up our clothes, prepared the beds, brought pails of washing water and bottles of drinking water, and filled the lamps with kerosene. Slept heavily and late for the first time since Meknès. Woke once in night to hear a great chorus of howling and barking below in the village. Lunch better than dinner last night, but everything was drowned in an inch of hot oil. *Tajne* of beef, almonds, grapes, olives and onions. Came back up to the hotel to make Nescafé on the terrace afterward. The old man who received us last night was sitting in a corner, buried under his *djellaba*. He saw we were looking at magazines, got up and came over. Soon he said timidly: "Is that an American book you are reading?" I said it was. He pointed to a colour photograph and asked: "And are the mountains in America really all green like that?" I told him many of them were. He stood a while studying the picture. Then he said bitterly: "It's not pretty here. The locusts eat the trees and all the rest of the plants. Here we're poor".

*

During the next few days I discovered how unrealistic my recording project had been. We visited at least two dozen villages in the region, and failed to discover an occasion where there might prove to be music. The previous year even the government had needed thirty-six hours' notice for sending its directives via a network of caids and messengers up into the heights, before the musicians had put in their appearance in Tafraout. When Friday morning arrived, Christopher said to me at breakfast: "What do you think? Do we leave tomorrow for Essaouira?" I said I supposed there was nothing else to do. Then I suggested we go down to the hospital to see if they had any Rovamycine.

A bearded Moroccan intern stood under a pepper tree in the hospital's patio, a syringe in his hand; he said the doctor had gone to Agadir for the weekend, but that if I wished I could speak with the French pharmacist, who, in the absence of his chief, was in charge of the institution.

The pharmacist arrived rubbing his eyes. He had been working all night, he told us. There was no Rovamycine. "It's an expensive drug. They don't supply us with that sort of thing here."

Christopher invited him to come up to the hotel for a whiskey.

"*Avec plaisir*," he said. Alcoholic drinks are not on sale in Tafraout. since Moslems cannot drink legally. The only two Europeans in the region were the doctor and the pharmacist, and they got by with an occasional bottle of wine or cognac they brought up from Tiznit.

The pharmacist had with him a young Moroccan medical student who had just arrived from Rabat the day before; he thought Tafraout the strangest place he had ever seen. We sat on the terrace in the scalding sun and watched the crows flying in a slowly revolving circle high above the valley. I was disappointed in my sojourn this time, I told Monsieur Rousselot, because I hadn't got into the life of the people and because there was no edible food. The second reason touched the Frenchman in him. "I shall do my best to fill these unfortunate lacunae," he said. "First let us go to my house for lunch. I have a good chef."

The house behind the hospital was comfortable. There were several servants. Walls were lined with books, particularly art books, for like many French men of medicine, Monsieur Rousselot loved painting, and had a hankering to try his hand at it himself one day.

During lunch he announced: "I have a little excursion in mind for this afternoon. Have you ever drunk *mahia*?" I said I had, many years ago, with Jewish friends in Fez. "Ah!" he exclaimed happily. "Then you are acquainted with its virtues. You will have an opportunity to drink *mahia* again later this afternoon." I smiled politely, having already determined that when the moment arrived I should decline the offer. I am not fond of *eau de vie*, even when it is made of figs, as it is in Fez. In the Anti Atlas they use dates, said Monsieur Rousselot; this doesn't seem an improvement.

After coffee and cognac, we started out down the Tiznit trail. Some thirty miles to the south, in a parched lower valley, we came to a poor-looking village called Tahala, which, besides its Moslem population, contains a Jewish colony of considerable size. The air was breathless as we got out of the car in front of the primitive little mosque. Five or six Moslem elders sat on the dusty rocks in the shade, talking quietly. "The Israelites add to their modest revenue by selling us the ambrosia they distill," explained Monsieur

Rousselot. Seddiq, the medical student, now expressed himself on the subject for the first time. "It's terrible!" he said with feeling. *"Bien sûr,"* agreed Monsieur Rousselot, "but you'll drink it."

Several children who had seen us arrive and park the car had run ahead into the village to announce our advent; now as we went along the oven-hot alleys, doors on all sides were being unceremoniously slammed shut and bolted. There was no one visible. But Monsieur Rousselot knew where he was going. He sent us ahead around the corner to wait out of sight while he pounded on one of the doors. It was a quarter of an hour before he reappeared and called to us. In the doorway where he had been standing talking stood an exceptionally pretty girl. The baby she held had an infected arm. Its forehead and nose were decorated in simple designs applied with kohl; one would have said that its face had been inexpertly tattooed. The room we went into was as dark and cool as a farmhouse cellar; the dirt floor slanted in various directions. A short flight of mud steps led up into an open patio with a well in its centre. Seven or eight very white-skinned women sat there on a bench around the well; they wore medieval head-dresses like those Tenniel gave the duchess in his illustrations for *Alice in Wonderland*. But they were all exceptionally handsome – even the old ones. No pictures could be taken, Monsieur Rousselot warned. The excuse they gave was that it was Friday afternoon. We were beckoned on into a further patio, this one full of men and boys, all wearing yamakas on their heads. From there we went into a small room with a brass bed at one end and a straw mat on the floor at the other. Asleep in the bed was a baby, naked and besieged by flies. We sat down on the mat in the sunlight, disturbing several hundred groggy flies; the men and boys came in from the patio one by one and solemnly shook hands with us. The big tray they put on the mat in front of us was piled high with almonds, dates, and flies both live and dead. Then the patriarch of the house was helped into the room by a younger man and eased into a sprawling position on the floor. His face was drawn and sad, and his replies to Monsieur Rousselot's questions were apathetic. "You must come to the hospital and let us examine you," urged

Monsieur Rousselot. The old man frowned and shook his head slowly. "They're all afraid," Monsieur Rousselot explained to me in French. "They consider the hospital a place where one goes to die, nothing more."

"Do you know what's wrong with him?" I asked.

"I'm almost certain it's the scourge."

"The scourge?"

"Cancer," snapped Monsieur Rousselot, as if the word itself were evil. "It carries them off, *whsht*, *whsht* . . ." He clicked his fingers twice.

Someone came and carried the baby away, still asleep. The flies remained behind. A small bottle of *mahia* was produced, and minature glasses of it were passed around. Surreptitiously I poured mine into Monsieur Rousselot's glass. Only the old man and I went without.

"He can't eat anything," explained one of the sons to Monsieur Rousselot. "Haven't you any pills for him?"

"Yes, yes, yes," said Monsieur Rousselot jovially, opening his doctor's bag. He took out two large jars, one filled with aspirin tablets, the other with Vitamin C pills, and poured a pile of them onto the mat. A murmur went around the patio, started by those who were crowding the doorway watching. "This is the only medicament I ever carry with me. It's all I have to give them. *Mais vous allez voir*. The pills will all stay behind here in Tahala." The flies crawled on our faces, trying to drink from the corners of our eyes. Monsieur Rousselot conferred quietly with one of the younger members of the family; presently two litre-bottles of *mahia* appeared and were packed into the medical bag. When we got up to leave, Monsieur Rousselot said to the old man: "Then it's agreed. You'll bring your grandson on Tuesday." To me he muttered: "Perhaps for the baby he'll come, and I can get him to stay for an examination. But it's doubtful."

Outside the front door a crowd of people had gathered. Word had got around that the *toubib* was there with his medicine. Monsieur Rousselot's prediction was accurate: there were not enough pills to go around.

On the way back up to Tafraout I said to him: "This has been an unforgettable day. Without it our trip to Tafraout would have been a failure." And I thanked him and said we would be leaving in the morning.

"Oh no! You can't go!" he cried. "I have something much better for you tomorrow."

I said we had to start moving northward.

"But this is something special. Something I discovered. I've never shown it to anyone before."

"It's not possible. No, no."

He pleaded. "Tomorrow is Saturday. Leave on Monday morning. We can spend tomorrow night in the palace and have Sunday morning for exploring the oases."

"Two days!" I cried. But the curiosity he had counted on awakening must have shown through my protestations. Before we left his house, I had agreed to go to Tassemsit. I could scarcely have resisted, after his description of the place. According to him, Tassemsit was a feudal town at the bottom of a narrow canyon, which by virtue of being the seat of an influential religious brotherhood had so far escaped coming under governmental jurisdiction, and was still functioning in a wholly traditional fashion. Absolute power was nominally in the hands of a nineteen-year-old girl, the present hereditary saint whose palace was inside the walls. In reality, however, said Monsieur Rousselot, lowering his voice to a whisper, it was the family chauffeur who held the power of life and death over the citizens of Tassemsit. The old Cherif, father of the girl-saint, for many years had run the *zaouia* where religious pilgrims came to pray and leave offerings. Not long ago he had bought a car to get up to Tafraout in now and then, and had hired a young Marrakchi to drive it. The old Cherif's somewhat younger wife, as wives sometimes do, had found the chauffeur interesting, and *"l'inévitable"* had happened: the old Cherif had suddenly died and the wife had married the young Marrakchi, who had taken charge of everything: the woman, the holy daughter, the car, the palace and the administration of the shrine and the town around it.

145

"It's an equivocal situation," said Monsieur Rousselot with relish. "You'll see."

*

Tassemsit, Sunday 16th. – Early morning. Others still asleep. Big grilled window right beside my head. A world of dappled sunlight and shadow on the other side of the wrought-iron filigree, an orchard of fig trees where small birds dart and chirp. Then the mud wall, and beyond, the stony floor of the canyon. A few pools of water in the river-bed. The women are out there, getting water, bringing it back in jugs. Background to all views: the orange sidewall of the canyon, perpendicular and high enough to block out the sky from where I sit on the mattress. More lurid details about the place from Rousselot yesterday during lunch. When the chauffeur took over, he instituted a novelty in Tassemsit: it seems he conceived the idea of providing girls to keep the pilgrims occupied at night, when the *zaouia* is closed. A great boost to the local economy. A holy city of sin, said Rousselot with enthusiasm. Merely speak to the chauffeur, and you get any woman in town, even if she happens to be married. Hardly finished telling us all this when a little fat man came in. Rousselot's face a study in chagrin, dropped jaw and all. He rallied then, introduced the little man around as Monsieur Omar, and made him sit down with us for coffee. Some sort of government employee. When he heard that we were about to leave for Tassemsit, Monsieur Omar said very simply that he would go with us. It was clear enough that he wasn't wanted, but since nobody said anything to the contrary, he came along, sitting in back with Monsieur Rousselot and Seddiq. Trail rough in spots on the way up over the peaks just south of Tafraout. Going down the other side it was narrower, but the surface was no worse. Had we met another car, one of us would have had to back up for a half-hour. The landscape became constantly more dramatic. For two hours the trail followed a valley that cut itself deeper and deeper into the rock walls as it went downward. Sometimes we drove along the bed of the stream for a half mile or so. At the date-palm level we came across small oases, cool and green, that filled the canyon floor from cliff to cliff. The lower we

146

went, the higher the mountain walls rose above, and the sunlight seemed to be coming from further away. When I was a child I used to imagine Persephone going along a similar road each year on her way down to Hades. A little like having found a back way out of the world. No house, no car, no human being all afternoon. Later, after we had been driving in shadow a good while, the canyon widened, and there on a promontory above a bend in the dry river-bed, was Tassemsit, compact, orange-gold like the naked rock of the countryside around it, still in the sunlight. A small rich oasis just below it to the south. The *zaouia* with its mosque and other buildings seemed to occupy a large part of the town's space. A big, tall minaret in northern style, well-preserved. We stopped and got out. Complete silence throughout the valley.

*

Monsieur Rousselot had seemed pensive and nervous all during the afternoon, and now I understood why. He got me aside on some pretext, and we walked together down the trail a way, he talking urgently the whole time. It worried him very much that Monsieur Omar should be with us: he felt that his presence repre-sented a very real danger to the status quo of the place. "One false move, and the story of Tassemsit can be finished forever," he said. "*C'est très délicat.*" Above all, not a word about what I told you. Any of it." I said he could count on me, and promised to warn Christopher. It came to me as we walked back up toward the car that there was probably another reason, besides the fact that he wanted to keep the place as his private playground, why Monsieur Rousselot was worried. A Frenchman's job in Morocco, if he works for the government, is never too secure in any case; it is easy to find a pretext which will dispose of him and replace him with a Moroccan. When we got to the car I spoke to Christopher, but he had already guessed the situation. At Monsieur Rousselot's insistence we waited another half hour; then we drove down a side trail to the right, to within two hundred feet of the town gate. A mist of sweet-smelling woodsmoke hung over the canyon. Several tall black men in white cotton robes appeared at the top of the rocks above us, came down to the car, and recognized Monsieur Rousselot.

Smiling, they led us through a short alley into the palace itself, small, primitive and elegant. The big room where they left us was a conscious synthesis of luxury and wild fantasy; with its irresponsible colour juxtapositions it was like something Matisse would have produced had he been asked to design a Moorish *salon*. "This is our room," said Monsieur Rousselot. "Here we are going to eat and sleep, the five of us." While we were unpacking, our host came in and sat down in our midst for a while. He was pleasant-mannered, quick-witted; he spoke a little French. A man in his late twenties, born in the country, I should say, but used to living in the city. At one point I became aware of the conversation he was having with Monsieur Rousselot, who had sat down beside him on the mattress. It concerned the possibility of an *ahouache*, performed by the citizens of Tassemsit later on in the evening. Afterward, when the host had left, Monsieur Rousselot announced that not only would we have the entertainment, but that there would be a certain number of women taking part in it. "Very unusual," he commented, looking owlishly at Monsieur Omar. Monsieur Omar grinned. "We are fortunate," he said; he was from Casablanca and might as well have been visiting Bali for all he knew about local customs. "You understand, of course," Monsieur Rousselot went on to say to me with some embarrassment, "this *ahouache* will have to be paid for."

"Of course," I said.

"If you and Monsieur Christopher can give three thousand, I should be glad to contribute two."

I protested that we should be delighted to pay the whole five thousand francs, if that was the price, but he wouldn't consider it.

Through the windows, from the silence in the canyon outside, came the thin sound of the muezzin's voice calling from the mosque, and as we listened, two light bulbs near the ceiling began to glow feebly. "It's not possible!" cried Christopher. "Electricity *here*?" "*Tiens*," murmured Monsieur Rousselot. "He's got his generator going at last." I looked wistfully up at the trembling filaments above my head, wondering whether the current and voltage might conceivably be right for recording. A tall servant came in and announced that the Cherifa was expecting us on the floor above. We filed out under the arcade and up a long flight of stairs. There at the top, on an open terrace, surrounded by roaring pressure-lamps, sat our host with two women. We were presented to the mother first. She would have been considered elegant anywhere in the world, with her handsome head, her regal white garments and her massive gold jewellery. The daughter, present titular ruler of Tassemsit, was something else; it was difficult to believe that the two had anything in common, or even that they inhabited the same town. The girl wore a pleated woollen skirt and a yellow sweater. She had had her front teeth capped with gold, and noisily snapped her chewing gum from time to time as she chatted with us. Presently our host rose and conducted us back down the stairs into our room, where servants had begun to arrive with trays and small tables.

It was an old-fashioned Moroccan dinner, beginning with soap, towels, and a big ewer of hot water. When everyone had washed and dried himself, an eathenware dish at least a foot and a half across was brought in and set in our midst; it held a mountain of couscous surrounded by a sea of sauce. We ate in the traditional manner, using our fingers, a process which demands a certain minimum of technique. The sauce was bubbling hot, and the tiny grains of semolina (since the cook knew his business) did not adhere to each other. Some of the food we extracted from the mound in front of us got to our mouths, but a good deal of it did not. I decided to wait a bit until someone had uncovered some of the meat buried in the centre of the mass, and when my opportunity came I seized a small piece of lamb which was still too hot to touch with comfort, but which I managed nevertheless to eat.

"I see that even the rudiments of local etiquette remain unknown to you," remarked Monsieur Rousselot to me in a voice which carried overtones of triumph rather than the friendly concern it might have expressed. I said I didn't know what he meant. "Have I committed an infraction?" I asked him. "Of the gravest," he said solemnly. "You ate a piece of meat. One is constrained to try some of every other element in the dish first, and even then one may not try the meat until one's host has offered one a piece of it with his own fingers."

I said this was the first time I had eaten in a home of the region. Seddiq, the medical student, observed that in Rabat such behaviour as Monsieur described would be considered absurd. But Monsieur Rousselot was determined to be an old Moroccan hand. "*Quelle décadence!*" he snorted. "The younger generation knows nothing." A few minutes later he upset a full glass of tea on the rug. "In Rabat we don't do that, either," murmured Seddiq.

Shortly after tea had been served for the third time, the electricity began to fail, and eventually it died. There was a pause in the talking. From where he sat, the head of the house shouted an order. Five white-dustered black men brought in candle-lanterns; they were still placing them in strategic positions around the room when the lights came on again, brighter than before. The lanterns were quickly blown out. Candles are shameful. Twenty minutes later, in the midst of a lion story (stories about lions are inevitable whenever city people gather in the country in South Morocco, although according to reliable sources the beasts have been extinct in the region for several generations), the current failed again, abruptly. In the silence of sudden darkness we heard a jackal yapping; the high sharp sound came from the direction of the river-bed.

"Very near," I remarked, partly in order to seem unaware of the host's probable embarrassment at having us witness the failure of his power system.

"Yes, isn't it?" He seemed to want to talk. "I have recorded them many times. Not one jackal – whole packs of them."

"You recorded them? You have a tape recorder here?"

"From Marrakech. It doesn't work very well. At least, not always."

Monsieur Rousselot had been busy scrabbling around his portion of the rug; now he suddenly lit a match and put it to the candle of the lantern near him. Then he stood up and went the length of the big room, lighting the others. As the patterns painted on the high ceiling became visible again, there was the sound of hand drums approaching from the town.

"The entertainers are coming," said our host.

Monsieur Rousselot stepped out into the courtyard. There was the increasing sound of voices; servants had appeared and were moving about beyond the doorway in the gloom. By the time we all went to look out, the courtyard had some fifty or sixty men in it, with more arriving. Someone was building a fire over in a corner under the far arcade. A drum banged now and then as its owner tested the membrane. Again the electricity came on. The master of the palace smiled at Monsieur Rousselot, disappeared, and returned almost immediately with a servant who carried a tape-recorder. It was a small model made by Philips of Holland. He set it up on a chair outside the doorway, and had great difficulty connecting it because none of the wall-plugs appeared to work. Eventually he found a live one. By that time there were more than a hundred men massed under the arches around the open centre of the courtyard, and in the middle were thirty or more musicians standing in an irregular circle. The host had propped the microphone against the machine. "Why not hang it up there on the wall?" I suggested.

"I want to talk into it once in a while," he said. When he turned the volume up the machine howled, of course, and there was laughter from the spectators, who until then had been very quiet, just standing and watching. The host had another chair brought, and he sat down in it, holding the microphone in his hand. Christopher caught my eye and shook his head sadly. More chairs were provided from out of the darkness, and someone arrived bringing a pressure-lantern, which was set inside the musicians' circle. That was where the fire ought to have been, but there was not enough space in the courtyard to put it there.

The performers, all Negroes, wore loose white tunics, and each carried a poignard in a silver scabbard at his waist. Their drums were the regulation *bendir*: a skin stretched over a wooden hoop about a foot and a half in diameter. This simple instrument is capable of great sonorous variety, depending on the kind of blow and the exact spot on the membrane struck by the fingertips or palm. The men of South Morocco do not stand still when they play the drums; they dance, but the purpose of their choreography is to facilitate the production of rhythm. No matter how involved or frenzied the body movements of the players, (who also sing in chorus and as soloists) the dancing is subordinate to the sound. It is very difficult to hear the music if one is watching the performance; I often keep my eyes shut during an entire number. The particular interest of the Anti-Atlas *ahouache* is that the drummers divide themselves into complementary groups, each of which provides only certain regularly recurring notes in the complex total of the rhythmical pattern.

The men began to play; the tempo was exaggeratedly slow. As they increased it imperceptibly, the subtle syncopations became more apparent. A man brandishing a *gannega*, a smaller drum with a higher pitch and an almost metallic sonority, moved into the centre of the circle and started an electrifying counter-rhythmic solo. His virtuoso drumbeats showered out over the continuing basic design like machine-gun fire. There was no singing in this prelude. The drummers, shuffling their feet, began to lope forward as they played, and the circle's counter-clockwise movement gathered momentum. The laughter and comments from our side of the courtyard ceased, and even the master of the palace, sitting there with his microphone in his hand, surrendered to the general hypnosis the drummers were striving to create.

When the opening number was over, there was a noisy rearranging of chairs. These were straight-backed and completely uncomfortable, no matter how one sat in them, and it seemed clear that no one ever used them save when Europeans were present. Few chairs are as comfortable as the Moroccan *m'tarrba* with its piles of cushions.

"Art Blakey'd enjoy this," said Christopher. "There's a lot of material here for him."

Our host leaned sideways, holding the microphone in front of his mouth, and said: *"Comment?"* Then he held it closer to Christopher for his reply.

"I was talking about a great Negro drummer in America."

He shifted it again. "Ah, yes. The Negroes are always the strongest."

Out in the open part of the courtyard groups of three or four men were going across into the far corner to tune their drums over the fire. Almost at once they began to perform; a long, querulous vocal solo was the prelude. One might have thought it was coming from the silence of the town, from somewhere outside the palace, it was so thin and distant in sound. This was the leader, creating his effect by standing in the darkness under the arches, with his face turned to the wall, as far away as he could get from the other performers. Between each strophe of his chant there was a long, profound silence. I became more aware of the night outside, and of the surperb remoteness of the town between the invisible canyon walls, whose only connection with the world was the unlikely trail we had rattled down a few hours earlier. There was nothing to listen for in the spaces between the plaintive cries, but everyone listened just the same. Finally, the chorus answered the far-away soloist, and a new rhythm got under way. This time the circle remained stationary, and the men danced into and out of the centre in pairs and groups, facing one another.

About halfway through the piece there was whispering and commotion in the darkness by the entrance door. It was the women arriving *en masse*. By the time the number was finished, sixty or seventy of them had crowded into the courtyard. During the intermission they squeezed through the ranks of standing men and seated themselves on the floor around the centre, bundles without form or face, wrapped in great dark lengths of cloth. Still, one could hear their jewellery clinking. One of them on my left suddenly rearranged her outer covering, revealing a magnificent turquoise robe embroidered in gold; then swiftly she became a sack of laundry once more. Several set pieces by the men followed, during which the women kept up a constant whispering among themselves; they watched politely, but it was evident that their minds were on the performance they themselves were about to give. When the men had finished and had retired from the centre, half the women present stood up and set about removing their outer garments. As they moved into the light they created a fine theatrical effect; the beauty of the scene, however, came solely from the variety of colour in the splendid robes and the flash of heavy gold adornments. There were no girls at all among them – which is another way of saying that they were all very fat. A curious phenomenon among female musicians in Morocco: at the beginning of their performance they seldom give much evidence of rythmic sense. This has to be worked up by the men playing the drums. At the outset they seem distraught, they talk and fidget, smooth their clothing, and seem interested in eveıything but the business at hand. It took a good deal of insistent drumming to capture the women on this occasion, but after two numbers the men had them completely. From then on the musical grew consistently more inspired. "*N'est-ce pas qu'elles-sont magnifiques?*" whispered Monsieur Rousselot. I agreed that they were wonderful; at the same time I found it difficult to reconcile what I was seeing with his earlier description of Tassemsit as a holy city of sin. Still, doubtless he knew best.

As the shrill voices and the drumming grew in force and excitement, I became convinced that what was going on was indeed extraordinarily good, something I should have given a good deal to be able to record and listen to later at my leisure. Watching my host in the act of idly ruining what might have been a valuable tape was scarecely a pleasure. Throughout their performance the women never stirred from where they stood, limiting their movements to a slight swaying of the body and occasional fantastic outbursts of antiphonal hand-clapping that would have silenced the Gypsies of Granada. With all that excess flesh, it was just as well they had no dance steps to execute. When the final cadence had died away, and while we applauded, they filed back to the shadows of the arcade and modestly wrapped their great cloths around them, to sit and listen to the *ahouache's* purely percussive coda. This was vigorous and brief; then a great crash of drums announced the end of the entertainment. We all stood up quickly, in considerable discomfort for having sat so long in the impossible chairs, and went back into the big room.

Five inviting beds had been made up along the mattresses at

intervals of perhaps twenty feet. I chose one in a corner by a window and sat down, feeling that I should probably sleep very well. The courtyard emptied in no time, and the servants carried away the chairs, the lantern and the tape-recorder. Monsieur Rousselot stood in the middle of the room, yawning as he took off his shirt. The host was shaking hands with each one of us in turn, and wishing us elaborate good-nights. When he came to me, he held out the flat box containing the tape he had just recorded. "A souvenir of Tassemsit," he said, and he bowed as he handed it to me.

The final irony, I thought. Of course, the spoiled tape has to be given to me, so that I can know in detail just what I failed to get. But my words to him were even more florid than his to me; I told him that it had been an unforgettable occasion, and that I was eternally indebted to him for this undeserved favour, and I wished him a pleasant night. Monsieur Omar was lying in his bed smoking, clad only in his shorts, a delighted and indestructible Humpty Dumpty. He was blowing smoke rings toward the ceiling. I did not feel that the future of Tassemsit was in immediate danger. Our host went out, and the door into the courtyard was shut behind him.

After everyone had gone to sleep, I lay there in the dark, listening to the jackals and considering my bad luck. Yet the original objective of the trip had been attained, a fact I discovered only when I got to the next place that had electricity. When I tried the tape in the hotel at Essaouira, fourteen out of its eighteen pieces proved to be flawless. There was no point in wondering why, since logically it was impossible; it had to be accepted as a joyful mystery. It is always satisfying to succeed in a quest, even when success is due entirely to outside factors. We bought blankets, trays, rugs and teapots, and set out again for the north.

GLOSSARY

ahouache   In the Grand Atlas and in territories to the south of it, a formalized festival involving groups of dancers, singers and percussionists.

benadir   Plural of *bendir*, a large disc-shaped drum with one membrane.

bidonvilles   The shantytowns that have grown up during the past three decades around the urban centres of North Africa. (The term is not geographically restrictive.)

chikh   The leader of a group of folk musicians.

comedor   The dining-room in a small hotel.

fraja   Mass dancing.

Guennaoua   (singular *Guennaoui*) A religious brotherhood, most of whose members are of Sudanese extraction, descendents of slaves. Their choreographed ritual is useful in the curing of madness, seizures and scorpion stings. They also rid houses of undesirable spirits.

katib   Secretary.

kif   The fine leaves at the base of the flowers of the common hemp plant, chopped and mixed (ideally in a ratio of seven to four) with tobacco grown in the same earth.

majoun   In North Africa *majoun* is the word for jam. Used in its special sense it is the word for any sweet preparation eaten with the purpose of including hallucinations, the active ingredient of which is the hemp plant.

medina   The Arabic word for city. In North Africa it indicates in particular that part of any city which was built by the Moslems and was already in existence at the time of the arrival of the Europeans.

meharistes   Saharan military cavalrymen mounted on trained camels.

Mouloud   The holiday commemorating the birthday of the Prophet Mohammed; also the month in which it occurs.

peloton   In French military usage, a detachment of soldiers.

qahouaji   In a small Moslem café the *qahouaji* prepares the tea and also serves it.

semolina   Grains made from grinding any cereal. In North Africa the process is slow: drops of water are sprinkled over the surface of flour, and the resulting accretions are shaken until they are globular and of the desired size.

souk   (properly *souq*) The word is used throughout North Africa to mean a market. In the larger cities it has a second, more specific use in designating a street or quarter devoted to the buying and selling (and often the manufacture) of one given commodity.

Spanioline Plural of *Spanioli*, a Spaniard.

toubib   Doctor.

tseuheur   The theory and practice of black magic.

zaouia   The seat of a religious brotherhood, generally comprising a mosque, a school, and the tomb of the sect's founder.

LET IT COME DOWN

Paul Bowles

Nelson Dyar has done something reckless. Not only has he thrown
up his boring but secure bank job in the States, but he has
ensconced himself in the unfamiliar world of Tangier's post-war
expatriate community, where his dubious sense of his own identity
makes him easy prey to intrigue and manipulation. Cast adrift on
a current of smuggling, espionage and murder, addled by hashish
and confused by sexual conundrums, he is swept into the morass of
curruption seething beneath Tangier's fashionable ennui.

Offered a chance to escape, Dyar takes it, fleeing to a lonely hut in
the mountains of Spanish Morocco. With drugs and isolation
fuelling his paranoia, he commits an act of terrifying violence
that liberates him – into a region of psychic disintegration and
horror . . .

0 349 10151 5
ABACUS FICTION

A THOUSAND DAYS FOR MOKHTAR

Paul Bowles

Stepping into the haunting dreamscapes of Latin America, Africa
or 'civilised' Manhattan as envisaged by Paul Bowles can lead to
wild and unnerving journeys: where chewing-gum machines form
part of a psychopath's armoury and a missionary in crisis falls
back on a scratchy 78 of 'Crazy Rhythm' to keep up church
attendance.

Revenge comes in many guises: cyanide in a parent's Piper
Heidsieck; gloating letters to a disliked stroke victim; amputation
of a linguistics professor's tongue. A restless evil spirit's greatest
satisfaction may be inhabiting the body of a young friar – until a
woman enters the remote valley monastery in question. With
disorienting, topsy-turvy logic two sisters may find themselves in
looking-glass lives – and butcher's bills can lead to murder . . .

0 349 10134 5
ABACUS FICTION

Abacus now offers an exciting range of quality fiction and non-fiction by both established and new authors. All of the books in this series are available from good bookshops, or can be ordered from the following address:

Sphere Books.
Cash Sales Department
P.O. Box 11
Falmouth
Cornwall TR10 9EN.

Please send cheque or postal order (no currency), and allow 60p for postage and packing for the first book plus 25p for the second book and 15p for each additional book ordered up to a maximum charge of £1.90 in U.K.

B.F.P.O. customers please allow 60p for the first book, 25p for the second book plus 15p per copy for the next 7 books, thereafter 9p per book.

Overseas customers including Eire please allow £1.25 for postage and packing for the first book, 75p for the second book and 28p for each subsequent title ordered.